A GUIDE TO

THE MEASUREMENT OF ANIMAL BONES

FROM ARCHAEOLOGICAL SITES

as developed by the Institut für Palaeoanatomie,
Domestikationsforschung und Geschichte der Tiermedizin
of the University of Munich

by

Angela von den Driesch

Peabody Museum Bulletin 1

Peabody Museum of Archaeology and Ethnology
Harvard University

1976

Information about available publications can be found at
www.peabody.harvard.edu/publications

COPYRIGHT © 1976 BY THE PRESIDENT AND FELLOWS OF HARVARD COLLEGE
ISBN 978-0-87365-950-5
LIBRARY OF CONGRESS CATALOG CARD NUMBER 76-49773
PRINTED IN THE UNITED STATES OF AMERICA

Second Printing 1977
Third Printing 1981
Fourth Printing 1995
Fifth Printing 1999
Sixth Printing 2004
Seventh Printing 2008
Eighth Printing 2010
Ninth Printing 2015

CONTENTS

INTRODUCTION TO THE SERIES

Publication has always been a valued part of the Peabody Museum's contribution to anthropological scholarship. In the Museum's first year, 1866, the annual report outlined progress on research projects, and these reports were soon augmented by occasional papers contributed by the staff. A more formal publication program was begun in 1888 with the *Peabody Museum Papers*, a series which has continued to be active for nearly ninety years.

The spectrum has been broadened through the years with the addition of the *Memoirs* and *Monograph* series, the *American School of Prehistoric Research Bulletins*, and the *Peabody Museum Press* publications. Each of the series was instituted to meet specific publishing requirements, but now a new need has become evident, and the *Peabody Museum Bulletin* is our response to it.

This inaugural volume of the *Bulletins* demonstrates the problem and the solution. Publishing costs for composition, printing, paper, and binding have reached a level that makes short runs of publications addressed to highly specialized audiences prohibitively expensive when traditional manufacturing processes are used. In order to make valuable information available to students and scholars, we are concentrating on efficiency and economy and are foregoing some of the niceties of book production that would increase prices more than anyone would like.

The *Bulletins* will add a useful flexibility to the Peabody's publication program. We are happy to add this volume and this series to our list.

Stephen Williams
Director
October 1976

FOREWORD

For the specialist in zooarchaeology, no foreword to this *Guide* is
really necessary. For the nonspecialist or student, however, and particularly for those from the English-speaking world, a few words of
introduction might be of value.

The purpose of publishing this *Guide* in English is to make available
to as wide an audience as possible the results of more than twenty years
of experience of the Munich school of osteoarchaeology in the taking of
measurements. The expectation is that the compilation will serve as a
standard to which future work will refer. Both the author of the *Guide*,
Dr. von den Driesch, and the director of the Institute for Palaeoanatomy,
Professor Boessneck, have expressed the desire that the reader clearly
understand that the measurement definitions published here are those
which workers in the Institute have found useful and which they hope
will be useful to others. "If they are useful, use them; if they are
not, change them," expresses their sentiments, qualified by the provision
that if different, the method of taking each dimension should be clearly
described. Thus, within clearly recognized limits, the hope is that
this *Guide* will be used as a handbook by faunal analysts working particularly in the Old World and will help to standardize the taking of measurements. Such standardization is essential if comparisons are to be
made between assemblages studied by different workers.

Although standardization of measurements is an important goal, it will
not be completely attainable, particularly for cranial material. Measurements taken for purposes of species identification need to conform to
those found useful by systematists. Such dimensions, however, may not
be suited to the description of variation resulting from the interaction
of human and animal populations. The measurement definitions presented
in this *Guide* are particularly useful for documenting dimensions which
reflect changes in the size and proportions of identified species. Additional or different measurements will need to be defined to distinguish
between closely related or similar species. In doing this, nonspecialists
should not only be acquainted with relevant literature, but also seek the
advice and guidance of knowledgeable zoologists. A danger of compilations
like this one is that they lend themselves to being used as "cookbooks"
with little consideration being given to the reasons why individual
dimensions are being measured.

A couple of other potential or actual shortcomings of the *Guide* should also be pointed out. In the first place, the present work deals primarily with the larger Holocene animals whose remains are commonly encountered in assemblages from European sites. The direct applicability of this compilation, therefore, is limited to Europe and the Near East, although its indirect utility, particularly as a guide to measurement of the post-cranial skeleton, extends to similar and related species throughout the world. Secondly, terms such as *greatest, smallest,* and *breadth* do not conform to the more common English *maximum, minimum,* and *width*. The author feels that closer approximations to the terminology used in the original German version of this *Guide* are preferable, particularly in the construction of abbreviations for postcranial dimensions. Although this point of view might be debated, it should be noted that all terms have been used in a consistent fashion throughout the work.

Finally, it is important to note that while the primary contribution of the *Guide* lies in its sixty-two figures and accompanying measurement definitions for both mammals and birds, the narrative portion of the work contains definitions and discussion which are indispensable to the proper use of this handbook in particular and of measurement data in general. A particularly important concept expressed both in the text and in Table 1 is that not all measurements are equal. Skeletal parts are recovered from archaeological sites in differing frequencies, are of varying value for the documentation of size, and are measurable with differing degrees of precision. All these factors affect the quality of the data collected and thus place limits on the nature and extent of possible interpretation. It is earnestly to be hoped that whenever measurements are taken, using this or any other guide, they will not be casually manipulated as abstract data, but will be carefully interpreted in the context of their particular element, species, site, area, and time period with due regard for biological and archaeological realities and for the strengths and limitations of this approach to documentation.

Richard H. Meadow
Peabody Museum
October 1976

PREFACE

This guide to the measurement of animal bones was originally developed
by Professor Joachim Boessneck and myself as part of the program of
instruction for students working on osteoarchaeological theses in the
Institute of Palaeoanatomy, Domestication Research, and History of
Veterinary Medicine of the University of Munich. During conferences of
osteoarchaeologists held in Budapest (1971) and in Groningen (1974), it
was suggested that I complete and distribute this measuring guide in
order to promote and standardize the taking of measurements of animal
bones recovered from prehistoric and early historic sites. The original
hope was for publication in various languages, but with the high cost
of printing, only this English version is to be published. The original
German text, however, is available in reduced xerographic form from the
Institute in Munich.

I thank the Director of the Institute, Professor Boessneck, for his
assistance in the preparation of this work. He in particular, because
of his long and varied experience in osteoarchaeology, is in a position
to judge a compilation of this kind. He aided me continually with
critical advice in the choice and definition of measurements and in
the arrangement of the diagrams. I thank him sincerely for his unremit-
ting help.

I likewise particularly thank the scientific draftsman of the Institute, Mr. R. Zluwa, for the preparation of the illustrations and for
marking in the measurements. He executed this tedious task with great
patience.

I am indebted to Dr. C. Grigson of the Odontological Museum in London
for translation of the introductory chapter and of the chapter on
the measurement of mammalian skulls. My translation of the second part of
the work was edited by Mrs. M. Fernando of Munich. Finally Mr. R.
Meadow of Cambridge, Massachusetts, reedited the complete manuscript
in preparation for publication. In addition, Dr. A. T. Clason of
Groningen and Dr. J. Clutton-Brock of London helped me by word and
by deed. My thanks to all.

Angela von den Driesch
Institut für Palaeoanatomie
September 1976

PART ONE

INTRODUCTORY STATEMENTS

INTRODUCTION

The measurement of bones that are to be scientifically studied is an essential part of their documentation. It is only when truly comparable measurements have been taken that it is possible to say anything objective about the size or form of the animal, to establish evolutionary lines, or to learn as much as possible about the history of the domesticated animals. (For further discussion, see Boessneck and von den Driesch 1976).

Among osteoarchaeologists working in Central Europe there is wide agreement that measurements must be taken on certain commonly occurring complete bones as well as on fragmentary specimens which are complete enough for certain dimensions to be taken. Furthermore, it is widely agreed that these measurements must be published in a clear and unambiguous form. One should measure not only skulls, teeth, toothrows, and complete long bones, but also the ends of long bones and the smaller bones such as those of the wrist, ankle, and foot. These last are usually very frequent in archaeological deposits and therefore can often be used to demonstrate the variation within an animal population better than the less numerous complete long bones. For most bones, more than one dimension should be taken in order to better elucidate the size and proportions of the animal.

The complete publication of single measurements is an expensive undertaking and usually has to be limited to essential information. Examples in the literature of the last ten years show how the documentation of bone finds can be done in an economical yet comprehensive fashion with the aid, for example, of diagrams and summarizing tables. It would take a whole chapter to go into all the possibilities. Here it is emphasized that for the primary publication of site material, the simplest and most objective presentation of the unprocessed metrical data is of primary importance. Only the least abstracted type of documentation can guarantee the use by others of the basic data in ways not envisioned or not pursued by the original analyst.

On the one hand, research completed early in the history of osteoarchaeology is largely out of date as far as interpretations are concerned. In so far as the early workers included measurement data, however, their publications can still form a valuable basis for modern osteoarchaeological research. On the other hand, there are numerous faunal analysts working on bone collections from parts of Europe and from the Near East who even up to the most recent times have failed to publish any measurement data, with the result that the value of their research is greatly reduced (e.g., Bataller 1952, 1953; Martín-Roldán 1959; Reed 1960; Hole and Flannery 1962; Perkins 1964). Other workers have published measurements, but too few and highly selective in nature (e.g., Ducos 1967; Hole, Flannery, and Neely 1969).

WHAT SHOULD BE MEASURED

The decision on which skeletal parts to measure and which measurements should be taken must in the end be made by each research worker for himself. The choice of measurement depends on the value of a find and on the aims of the research. No norm can be set for the specialist. However, if we hope, from the point of view of universal validity, to achieve comparable results, the use of the same measurements is of the greatest importance in original research on site refuse.

The following bones and parts of bones should be measured:

1) Complete skulls, larger skull fragments, mandibles, toothrows, and single cheek teeth (so long as they are identifiable). The following teeth should be measured individually in the case of the common domestic animals:

   Equids: P^2-M^3 and P_2-M_3*
   Ruminants: M_3
   Pigs: M^3 and M_3
   Carnivores: $P^4(-M^2)$ and $M_1(-M_3)$.

2) Complete long bones as well as the phalanges of digitigrades (carnivores and lagomorphs) which, however, should be measured only when their exact radial position in the hand or foot can be established. The articular ends of long bones should also be measured.

3) Patellae, larger wrist and ankle bones, and the distal sesamoid bone of equids.

4) The first two cervical vertebrae and the sacrum as well as any vertebrae between them whose exact serial position in the vertebral column can be established.

5) The penis bone of carnivores.

Bones that have been in a fire and subjected to high temperatures or calcined become smaller to an extent which depends upon the degree of influence of the heat. To obtain an idea of the extent of the size (and weight) loss, the following experiment was conducted by the author together with H. J. Gregor of the Anthropological Institute of the University of Munich: single skeletal parts of the right and left sides of the bodies of different wild and domesticated animals were measured and weighed. The bones of the right side then were heated for one hour at a temperature of 850° C., and those of the left side were heated for one hour and twenty minutes at a temperature of 1000° C. in a muffle oven. As a result of treatment, the bones of the right side turned black, and on average they had lost 5% of their size and c. 50% of their weight. The bones of the left side turned white, were on the average 15% smaller, and had also lost 50% of their weight. For example, the lateral length of both astragali of a wild pig before heating was 40.5 mm; following the experiment, the measurement of the right astragalus was 38.5 mm and of the left 34.5 mm. (See also Iregren and Jonsson 1973.)

---

*The teeth are numbered and designated as follows:

$I^1, I^2, I^3, C, P^1, P^2, P^3, P^4, M^1, M^2, M^3$ Upper Jaw

$I_1, I_2, I_3, C, P_1, P_2, P_3, P_4, M_1, M_2, M_3$ Lower Jaw

I = Incisor, C = Canine, P = Premolar; M = Molar.

The results of the heating experiment suggest, therefore, that carbonized and calcined bones should not be measured; if measurements are taken, they are of only limited use. In addition, bones that are pathologically or anatomically abnormal are only measurable in a limited way and have to be interpreted specially case by case.

In general, only the bones of full grown animals should be measured; in the young animal an increase in size has to be allowed for and the resulting corrected measurement is not precise enough to permit an accurate estimation of size. The measurement of bones that are known to be from young animals can only be justified in the case of exceptional size or in the study of particular age groups (see von den Driesch and Boessneck 1970; Boessneck and von den Driesch 1973, p. 19 and table 13). If bones of young animals are measured, these have to be specially designated.

In the case of slaughter refuse, with its numerous bone fragments, it is not possible in every case to estimate the exact age of the animal from which one particular bone derived. Because the epiphysal union of the proximal and distal ends of long bones can take place at different ages, when broken ends of long bones are examined one often cannot determine whether they belonged to fully grown animals or to animals that were still young at the time of slaughter. For example, in order to be sure that only tibiae from full grown animals are being measured, only tibiae with both proximal and distal epiphyses fused should be measured. Such a procedure will, of course, considerably reduce the number of measurable bones, since complete tibiae are rare in slaughter refuse. For this reason all fused distal tibiae should be measured, even though some may not have fused proximally. In the case of ungulates, proximal epiphyses fuse about one and one-half years after the distal epiphyses (Zietzschmann 1924, Silver 1963). During this period an animal can still grow considerably.

The distal epiphysis of the tibiae fuses to the diaphysis at the end of the second or during the course of the third year in most domestic animals, by which time the animal has already passed its phase of most rapid growth. At this age the inclusion of dimensions of certain bones like the distal tibia, which come from animals whose immaturity cannot be recognized, will have less impact on the statistical results than will the inclusion of measurements of other bones whose epiphyses have already fused in the first year of life, e.g., the scapula. This situation suggests that not all bones whose articular ends are measured have the same usefulness for the estimation of size because under one category of articular ends young animals could be included in greater numbers than under another.

Epiphysal sutures are still visible for rather a long time after the actual fusion takes place, the region of fusion being dotted with large pores. Articular ends of the early fusing elements which bear such telltale signs should not be measured. For skeletal parts that have no sutures, like the astragalus, one can use the degree of compactness of the bone as a criterion of age. Bones of young animals are more porous, their structure is more spongy, and they are lighter than bones from fully grown animals. None of these characters can be used with certainty, however, so that the measurement of bones from young animals cannot be avoided altogether.

In the refuse of prehistoric and early historic sites, certain skeletal parts of the commonly kept animals are especially frequent, while others are less common, and still others are seldom found. These different frequencies result from the fact that the bones of prehistoric and early historic sites were shattered in varying degrees and to the fact that certain parts of the skeleton preserve better than others. So one finds, for example, only a few of the larger limb bones of the common food animals because these bones usually were broken open by the inhabitants of the more ancient sites in order to obtain the marrow. The large long bones of equids and of the smaller ungulates, however, are often better preserved than those of cattle and red deer whose bones were much more intensively utilized. In the case of the small domestic animals, complete long bones of sheep and goat predominate over those of pigs because the use of pigs exclusively for food almost invariably led to their slaughter at a young age. The bones of young animals are less resistant to soil conditions than are the bones of fully grown animals.

Of the horned animals, the horncores of goats are more durable than those of cattle and sheep which tend to disintegrate because of their greater porosity and crumbly consistency. One therefore gets relatively more measurements from the horncores of goats than from those of cattle or sheep.

Complete toothrows of small hoofed mammals are more often measurable than those of the large ungulates because large skulls are more likely to have been broken up for marrow. For similar reasons, short bones generally are better preserved than the larger long bones. If such bones fall below a certain size, however, they are more easily overlooked in an excavation where sieving is not carried out. Because of this, measurements of the short bones of large animals are taken more often than those of small animals.

The proximal and distal ends of broken long bones are also preserved in differing frequencies. Measurable ends of those long bones whose epiphyses fuse at an early age (such as the distal humerus and the proximal radius) occur in greater numbers because the bone consolidates earlier. Ends whose epiphyses fuse later (such as the proximal humerus and the distal radius) tend to be less frequent not only because not all animals of a population are permitted to complete growing before they are slaughtered, but also because the wall of the bone is less compact and thus less resistant to destructive forces. Such bones are therefore less frequently available for measurement. Ultimately, of course, the preservation of a bone depends also on the structure of the spongy bone and on the direction and concentration of its lines of stress.

All of the above considerations must be taken into account during the evaluation of measurements of each part of the skeleton. Table 1 brings together this information for each measurable component of the skeletons of the more important hoofed mammals.

TABLE 1:   *Relative values of the measurable skeletal parts of the*
            common hoofed mammals.

KEY: <u>Frequency</u>:   o = almost none
                        x = rare
                       xx = moderately frequent
                      xxx = frequent

        <u>Relative value</u> of the measurement for size estimation:

        <u>postcranial skeleton</u>:

            1 = <u>very good</u>, because the bone certainly came from a fully
                grown animal.

            2 = <u>good</u>, because the bone came from an animal whose age can
                be determined from epiphysal fusion to have been 2 - 3
                years old and which therefore had attained nearly full
                adult size.

            3 = <u>moderate</u>, because among the measured bones there may be
                those from animals aged 1 - 2 years.

            4 = <u>slight</u>, because among the measured bones there may be
                those of animals aged less than 1 year.

        <u>skull</u>:

            All skull measurements have the value '1' because one measures
            only those skulls and skull fragments which come from animals
            that reached the age of complete permanent dentition and so
            would have shown no more real growth. (Exception: detached
            horncores cannot be used unless the age of the animal can be
            established.)

        <u>Measurability</u>:

            + = the measurements are clear and easy to take.
            - = the measurements are difficult to take.

        <u>Animal species</u>:   E = Equid
                            B = <u>Bos</u>
                            S = <u>Sus</u>
                          O/C = <u>Ovis</u>/<u>Capra</u>

NOTES: 1) Only <u>Bos</u>.
          2) Only <u>Ovis</u> and <u>Capra</u>. The horncores of goat are usually more
             frequent than those of sheep.
          3) The relative value depends upon whether the epiphysal fusion
             of the tuber olecrani can be ascertained.

TABLE 1

SKELETAL PART	FREQUENCY hoofed mammals large	small	RELATIVE VALUE hoofed mammals large	small	MEASURABILITY hoofed mammals large	small
complete SKULL	o	o	1	1	+/-	+/-
HORNCORE	x[1]	xx[2]	3	3	+	+
MAXILLA: complete toothrow	o-x	x-xx	1	1	+/-	+/-
MANDIBLE: complete toothrow	x	xx-xxx	1	1	+/-	+/-
single M3	xx	xxx	1	1	+/-	+/-
ATLAS, AXIS	x	x	2	2	+	+
SCAPULA, whole	o	o	3	3	+	+
distal	xx	xx	3	3	+	+
HUMERUS, whole	o	x	1	1	+/-	+/-
proximal	x	x	1	1	+/-	+/-
distal	xx	xxx	3	3	-	-
RADIUS, whole + distal	x	x-xx	1	1	+	+
proximal	xxx	xxx	3	O/C:4 S:3	+	+
ULNA, proximal	xx	O/C:x S:xxx	1/4[3]	1/4[3]	-/+	-/+
PELVIS, whole	o	x	1	1	+	+
acetabulum	xx	xx	4	4	-	-
FEMUR, whole + distal	B:o E:x	x	1	1	+ +/-	+
proximal	x	xx	1	1	+	+
PATELLA	x	x	4	4	+	+
TIBIA, whole+proximal	x	x-xx	1	1	+	+
distal	xx-xxx	xx-xxx	2	2	+	+
CALCANEUS	x	x	2	2	+	+
ASTRAGALUS	xxx	xx	4	4	E:- B:+	+
ruminant CENTROTARSALE	xx	x	4	4	+	+
whole and distal METAPODIALS	xx	xx	E:3 B:2	O/C:3 S:2	+	+
proximal METAPODIALS	xxx	xxx	4	4	+	O/C:+ S:+/-
PHALANX 1	xxx	xx	E:3 B:2	O/C:4 S:2	+/-	+/-
PHALANX 2	xxx	x-xx	3	O/C:4 S:3	+/-	+/-
PHALANX 3	xx	x	4	4	E:- B:+	+

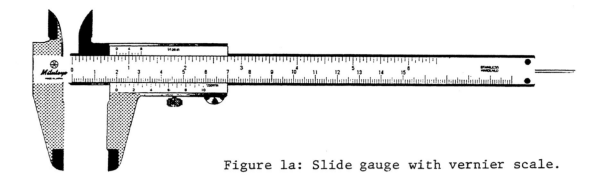

Figure 1a: Slide gauge with vernier scale.

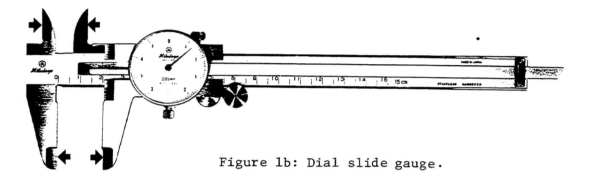

Figure 1b: Dial slide gauge.

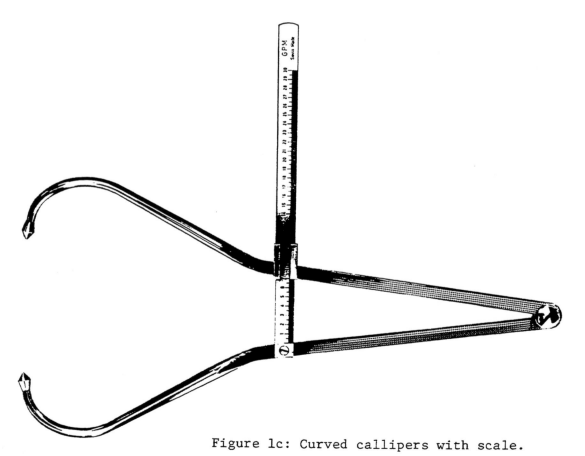

Figure 1c: Curved callipers with scale.

MEASUREMENTS AND MEASURING INSTRUMENTS

Measurements are given in millimeters, and only exceptionally in centimeters. For the longer dimensions (the bones of larger animals) the measurements are given to the nearest 0.5 mm and for the shorter dimensions (bones of small mammals, birds, reptiles, and amphibians) to the nearest 0.1 mm.

Usually the measurements are taken with a slide gauge fitted with a vernier scale (Fig. 1a). A modification of this is the dial slide gauge which is calibrated in millimeters and tenths of millimeters (Fig. 1b). This type of scale has the advantage that the eye does not tire so quickly when a large series of measurements is being taken. When projections of bone hinder the taking of measurements with a slide gauge, one has to use curved callipers equipped with a scale (Fig. 1c) to reach both measuring points.

In this regard, two automatic measuring apparati developed independently by Gejvall (1973) in Stockholm and Dolling and Reichstein (1975) in Kiel are of interest. The advantage of such apparatus is that reading and recording mistakes are eliminated; individual measurements are automatically recorded and punched onto perforated tape which then can be interpreted by computer.

For many bones the use of a measuring box is helpful (Fig. 2). Such a device is suitable for taking dimensions for which the two measuring points do not lie in the same plane and for which the dimensions must be measured in projection (e.g., the distal end of the femur in large animals, the greatest breadth of the astragalus in the horse, and the greatest length of the first phalanx in the horse). In many such cases, however, a slide gauge with long and wide arms can be successfully employed.

For the measurement of circumferences and curves (of horncores and diaphyses of long bones) one uses a tape measure or a smooth thread that is neither too thick nor too thin and which is marked and then laid on a scale. Such measurements can be made only to the nearest millimeter.

When a bone is slightly damaged the complete length or breadth can be estimated and recorded in brackets. The only purpose of recording the actual measurement is as a check on the estimated measurement.

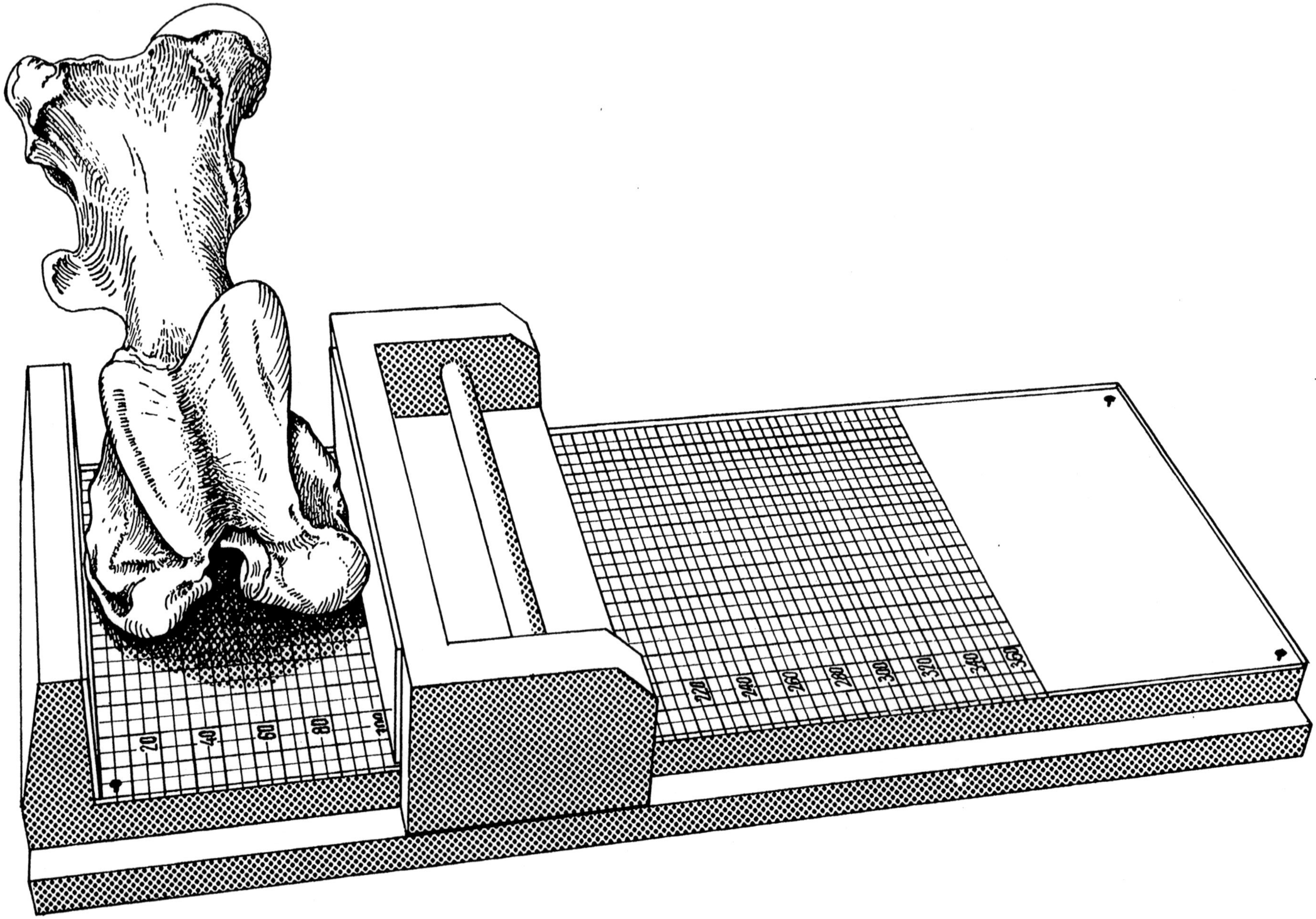

Figure 2: Measuring Box.

THE TAKING OF MEASUREMENTS

In the taking of measurements there will always be discrepancies from one research worker to the next which will influence the final results. Even one and the same person may not always work in the same way. Anyone who has measured bones knows that merely to measure the bones of the right and left sides in the same way is difficult enough. Discrepancies occur, however, primarily because, regardless of the true dimensions, some bones are less precisely measurable than others (see also Table 1). Here are some examples: most measurements of the skull can be taken without difficulty because they can be taken from easily defined fixed points (see below under "Skull: Cranium"). Where necessary one can mark these points on the actual skull itself. Also for most of the long bones one can measure length and often breadth (width) with hardly any inaccuracy (e.g., greatest proximal breadth of radius and, in horses and ruminants, greatest distal breadth of metapodials, lengths of the astragalus, etc.), and such measurements are unrestrictedly comparable.

The situation is different with single teeth. One usually finds in the literature that the "length" and "breadth" (width) of the single teeth of herbivores are measured "near to the biting surface." The use of the term "near to" is very subjective: one person may measure farther up and another farther down. Furthermore, there is a difference between the measurements of loose teeth and those which are fixed in a jaw and which cannot be removed without damaging the bone. The pointers of the measuring instrument can be fixed easily on loose teeth; one finds that with teeth that are still in their sockets the measuring instruments cannot reach the same points. One manipulates them until one thinks that one has made approximately the same measurement as on loose teeth. These circumstances, however, generally mean that one uses a different standard for teeth in sockets than for loose teeth.

A number of such inconsistencies will be apparent to the user of the present work. In order to give at least some indication of such difficulties, in the following pages the sign "+" is given for dimensions which are precisely measurable and the sign "-" for dimensions which are less precisely measurable. It is not, however, the purpose of the present work to eliminate all imprecisions. It is simply not possible to arrive at an exact, infallible definition for every dimension. Our intention here is to demonstrate that one must oneself be clear about the occurrence of inexactitudes and that one must bear in mind this state of affairs in any subsequent comparisons with measurements given in the literature. In order to be quite certain, one should use only the "good" (precisely measurable) dimensions to arrive at a true picture. Given this advice, the question arises whether it would not be more appropriate to leave out the measurements that are difficult to take (e.g., the distal breadth [width] of the humerus in ruminants, the greatest breadth of the astragalus in equids or all dimensions of the proximal ulna) as many authors have in fact done. We believe that the omission of skeletal measurements that are difficult to take accurately should not be made a rule because among those bones there are some whose dimensions are very important for the estimation of size, for example the teeth and the phalanges. In conclusion, it may be said that in large samples these inaccuracies even themselves out as is shown when the size changes of cattle in Europe are worked out from measurements available in the literature (Boessneck et al. 1971, pp. 56 ff.).

In the following pages the definitions of measurements for crania, mandibles, teeth, vertebrae, and limb bones of both common mammals and birds—the result of more than twenty-five years of experience of the Munich school of osteoarchaeology—have been brought together. These definitions are explained partly by diagrams and partly by short descriptions. This arrangement has been made primarily for beginners and inexperienced research workers. It is also intended to be used as a "Field Guide" for bone measurement, particularly on excavation sites where literature may be lacking.

PART TWO

MEASUREMENT OF THE MAMMALIAN SKELETON

GENERAL

The most important introduction to the measurement of bones is Duerst's
work of 1926: "Vergleichende Untersuchungsmethoden am Skelett bei Säugern."
Duerst gathered together all the information on the measurement of skulls
and limb bones of mammals that existed in the literature at that time,
and he clearly defined the measurements and measuring points. Many of
these, particularly those of the skull, are still named and selected in
the same way. His selection of measurements, however, goes far beyond
the needs of osteoarchaeology, and the special requirements of this dis-
cipline are not always recognized. The measurements defined by Duerst
are extremely numerous, but experience has shown that only a few well-
defined dimensions need be measured in order to estimate size and proportions
from bones recovered from archaeological deposits. Nevertheless Duerst's
work remains very important as an introduction and for specialized
research of other kinds.

The assembling of measurements from the practical experience gained
during the course of research by Hescheler's school (see Boessneck 1969,
pp. 49 ff.), particularly in Kuhn's dissertation (1932), influenced the
methodological development of comparative osteology almost more than
did Duerst's great theoretical work. The precise definition, however,
of these subsequently widely-used measurements, and of newly introduced
additional measurements, has been lacking until now. For even if similar
sets of measurements are now generally used in the osteoarchaeological
research of German-speaking workers, differences still do exist with the
result that comparability of results suffers. It is high time for methods
to be standardized in detail.

In order to define measurements it is important to know how to denote
the directions and planes of the animal body. Unfortunately such nomenclature differs in zoological, veterinary, and medical textbooks.

(Compare, for example, Romer 1971, pp. 9 ff. with Ellenberger and Baum 1943, pp. 1 ff. and Nickel, Schummer, and Seiferle 1961, p. 7. Anthropology uses other directional nomenclature as well.) I propose to use the nomenclature that is set out in Figures 3 and 4 in order to overcome the lack of standardization. The direction toward the plane of support (the ground) is termed *ventral* and the opposite direction is *dorsal* (or *frontal*). The *median plane* divides the body longitudinally into similar halves. Planes parallel to the median plane are *paramedian* or *sagittal*. A surface which is nearer than another to the median plane is *medial* to it and a surface which is farther than another from the median plane is *lateral* to it. The direction toward the head is termed *cranial* and toward the tail *caudal,* with the front and back sides of the scapula, humerus, pelvis, and femur designated accordingly. With respect to parts of the head, the corresponding terms are *oral* and *nasal* directed toward the mouth and nose with the opposite being *aboral* or *nuchal*.

The definitions of *dorsal* and *volar* (or *palmar*) in the forelimb and *dorsal* and *plantar* in the hind limb, derive, like many other expressions, from human anatomy, and come from *dorsum manus* and *dorsum pedis* (the back of the hand and of the foot), *vola* (or *palma*) *manus* and *planta pedis* (the palm of the hand and the sole of the foot, respectively). These terms can be used in animals for all the limb bones below the elbow and knee. *Proximal* and *distal* express relative directions in the long axis of the limbs. It also must be noted in the cases of horncores, antlers, and tail bones that the direction toward the tip is designated as *distal* and toward the head or toward the body as *proximal*.

Linear measurements are designated as *length, breadth* (width), *depth, or height*. It is necessary to pay strict attention to the following definitions:

<u>Length</u> a) for all bones of the axial skeleton and of the pectoral and pelvic girdles is that dimension measured in a cranio-caudal direction.

        b) for all bones of the remaining appendicular skeleton is that dimension measured in a proximo-distal direction.

<u>Breadth</u> (width) on all bones is that dimension measured in a medio-lateral direction.

<u>Height</u> for all bones of the skull, of the axial skeleton, and of the pectoral and pelvic girdles is that dimension measured in a dorso-ventral direction.

<u>Depth</u> for all bones of the extremities is that dimension measured in a cranio-caudal direction (i.e., dorso-volar or dorso-plantar).

Measurements that do not lie in any one of the three basis directions are designated as *diagonals* or *diameters*.

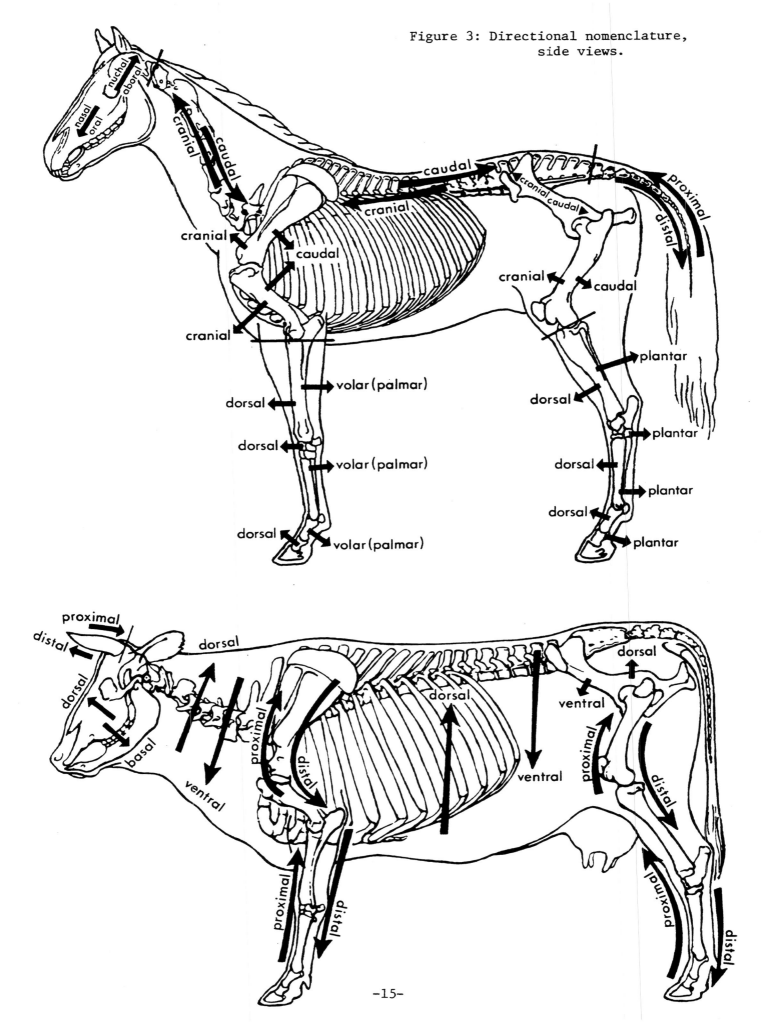

Figure 3: Directional nomenclature, side views.

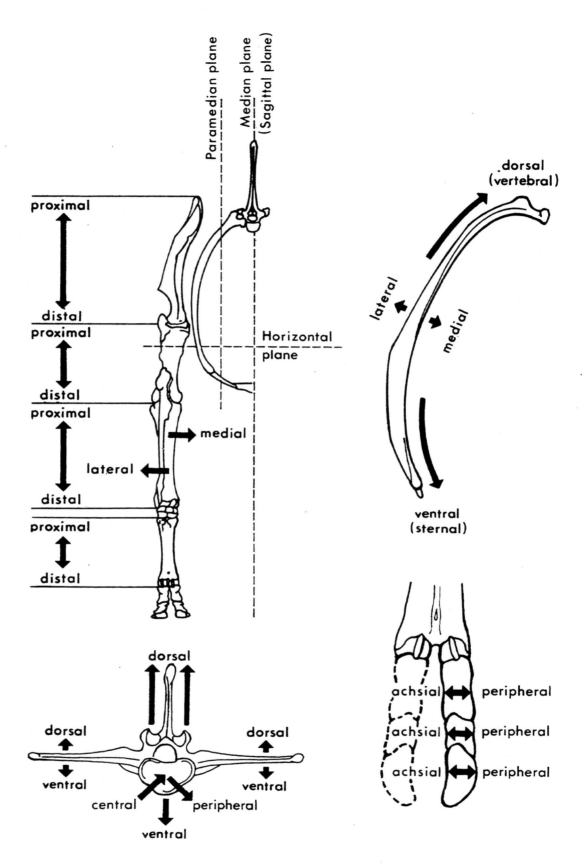

Figure 4: Directional nomenclature,
fore and aft views.

SKULL

CRANIUM

All individually important measuring points that are used in the text and in the illustrations are defined following Duerst (1926, pp. 237 ff.). Some remarks, however, on the points *opisthokranion and akrokranion* are necessary. According to Duerst (ibid.), the opisthokranion is "the most aboral point on the skull vertex" and the akrokranion is "the most aboral and highest point that lies in the median plane." Length measurements taken from the opisthokranion, according to Duerst, would obviously be measured from a point that is not actually in the median plane and so would have to be measured in projection (Duerst 1926, Figs. 108 and 109). Of the animals being considered here, in camels, sheep, goats, red deer, dogs, cats, and hares the opisthokranion and the akrokranion coincide (also Duerst 1926, Fig. 107). In horses and cattle the two points are only a few millimeters apart and hence we propose that in those two species length measurements should be taken from the akrokranion, there being scarcely any difference between measurements taken from the two points. A fixed point on the skull can be comprehended more easily than one that has to be projected into the median plane and thus is situated in space. In the pig, however, the opisthokranion and the akrokranion are situated significantly farther apart from one another because the nuchal crest is drawn out more or less aborally depending on the type of pig. Thus for the pig it is very important to note that the two points are quite clearly distinct.

For anatomical terms such as *foramen magnum* which are used in the definitions of measuring points, reference is made to Nickel, Schummer, and Seiferle (1961) and to Sisson and Grossman (1950). Please also note that before measuring it is advisable to mark on the skull all those points that are defined by the intersection with the median plane of a line joining two points.

Definitions of measuring points of the cranium

A   - Akrokranion, the most aboral point on the vertex of the cranium in the median plane.
B   - Basion, the orobasal border of the foramen magnum in the median plane.
Br - Bregma, the median point of the parieto-frontal suture.
Ect - Ectorbitale, the most lateral point of the frontal bone on the occipital side of the orbit.
Ent - Entorbitale, the naso-medial indentation of the orbit that corresponds with the inner angle of the eye in the living animal.
Eu - Euryon, the most lateral point of the braincase.
F   - Frontal midpoint, the median point of the line joining the Ectorbitalia (only in carnivores).
H   - Hormion, the aboral border of the vomer in the median plane.
If - Infraorbitale, the (dorso) aboral point of the foramen infra-orbitale.
L   - Lambda, the median point of the parieto-occipital suture.
N   - Nasion, the median point of the naso-frontal suture.

Ni - Nasointermaxillare, the most aboral point of the premaxilla on the facial surface.
O - Opisthion, the nuchodorsal border of the foramen magnum in the median plane.
Op - Opisthokranion, the median point of the line joining the most aboral-dorsal points of the cranium.
Ot - Otion, the most lateral point of the mastoid region (in cattle, red deer, and dogs this is dorsal to the opening of the external auditory meatus, in horses, camels, sheep, goats, and cats it is occipital to the meatus; in pigs it is on the opening of the meatus).
P - Prosthion, the median point of the line joining the most oral points of the premaxillae. In all ruminants and in pigs the prosthion has to be projected into space. At best one can use one pointer of the slide gauge to fix the most oral point of the two premaxillae.
Pd - Postdentale, the median point of the line joining the aboral points of the alveoli of the hindmost cheekteeth.
Pm - Premolare, the median point of the line joining the oral points of the alveoli of the foremost cheekteeth.
Po - Palatinoorale, the median point of the palatine-maxillary suture.
Rh - Rhinion, the median point of the line joining the most oral points of the nasals.
S - Synsphenion, the midpoint of the suture between the basisphenoid and the presphenoid (= Intersphenoidsuture).
Sp - Supraorbitale, the median point of the line joining the aboral borders of the supraorbital foramina.
St - Staphylion, the most aboral point of the horizontal part of the palate in the median plane.
Zy - Zygion, the most lateral point of the zygomatic arch.

Tooth formulae of the different species (upper/lower jaws):

Equus	$\dfrac{3.\ 1.\ (4)\ 3.\ 3}{3.\ 1.\ 3.\ 3}$	Canis	$\dfrac{3.\ 1.\ 4.\ 2}{3.\ 1.\ 4.\ 3}$
Camelus	$\dfrac{1.\ 1.\ 3.\ 3}{3.\ 1.\ 2.\ 3}$	Felis	$\dfrac{3.\ 1.\ 3.\ 1}{3.\ 1.\ 2.\ 1}$
Bos, Ovis and Capra	$\dfrac{0.\ 0.\ 3.\ 3}{3.\ 1.\ 3.\ 3}$	Ursus	$\dfrac{3.\ 1.\ 4\text{-}1.\ 2}{3.\ 1.\ 4\text{-}1.\ 3}$
Cervus	$\dfrac{0.\ 1.\ 3.\ 3}{3.\ 1.\ 3.\ 3}$	Lepus and Oryctolagus	$\dfrac{2.\ 0.\ 3.\ 3}{1.\ 0.\ 2.\ 3}$
Sus	$\dfrac{3.\ 1.\ 4.\ 3}{3.\ 1.\ 4.\ 3}$		

Measurements of the cranium of Equus (Figs. 5a,b,c,d and 6a,b)

1) Profile length = total length: Akrokranion - Prosthion (+)
2) Condylobasal length: aboral border of the occipital condyles - Prosthion (+)
3) Basal length: Basion - Prosthion (+)
3a) Basilar length: Basion - the point between the two I^1 (difficult to measure when the incisors cannot be removed from the jaw)
4) Short skull length: Basion - Premolare (+)
5) Basicranial axis: Basion - Hormion (-)
6) Basifacial axis: Hormion - Prosthion (+)
*(7) Neurocranium length: Basion - Nasion. Not shown in Fig. 5. Can be taken only with curved callipers (+)
8) Viscerocranium length: Nasion - Prosthion (+)
9) Upper neurocranium length: Akrokranion - Supraorbitale (+)
10) Facial length: Supraorbitale - Prosthion (+)
11) Basion - most oral point of the facial crest on one side (+)
12) Most oral point of the facial crest on one side - Prosthion (+)
13) Short lateral facial length: Entorbitale - Prosthion (+)
14) Length of braincase: Opisthion - Ectorbitale (+)
15) Lateral facial length: Ectorbitale - Prosthion (-)
16) Greatest length of the nasals: the median point of intersection of the line joining the aboral borders of the nasals - Rhinion (+ except in old horses in which the fronto-nasal sutures are obliterated)
17) Basion - Staphylion (-)
18) Median palatal length: Staphylion - Prosthion (+)
18a) Palatal length: the median point of intersection of the line joining the deepest indentations of the choanae - Prosthion (-)
19) Dental length: Postdentale - Prosthion (+)
20) Lateral length of the premaxilla: Nasointermaxillare - Prosthion (-)
21) Length of the diastema (P^2-I^3) (+)
22) Length of the cheektooth row (measured along the alveoli) (+)
22a) Length of the cheektooth row (measured near the biting surface) (+)
23) Length of the molar row (measured along the alveoli on the buccal side (-)
23a) Length of the molar row (measured near the biting surface) (-)
24) Length of the premolar row (measured along the alveoli on the buccal side (-)
24a) Length of the premolar row (measured near the biting surface) See Fig. 6a (-)

*Measurement numbers which do not appear in the figures are enclosed in full parentheses - "( )".

25)	Length and breadth of P^2	The form of the biting surface is very
26)	Length and breadth of P^3	variable in <u>Equus</u> and is particularly
27)	Length and breadth of P^4	dependent on the degree of wear. For
28)	Length and breadth of M^1	the length measurement (except for M^3)
29)	Length and breadth of M^2	the most aboral points of the aboral
30)	Length and breadth of M^3	contact surface are the fixed points
		from which to measure.

In M^3 the most oral points of the oral contact surface are used.
For breadth measurements one always uses the most buccal points
of the cheektooth as the fixed points (Fig. 6b).

31) Greatest inner length of the orbit: Ectorbitale - Entorbitale (+)
32) Greatest inner height of the orbit. Measured in the same way as M 31 (+)
33) Greatest mastoid breadth: Otion - Otion (+)
34) Greatest breadth of the occipital condyles (+)
35) Greatest breadth at the bases of the paraoccipital processes (+)
36) Greatest breadth of the foramen magnum (+)
37) Height of the foramen magnum: Basion - Opisthion (-)
38) Greatest neurocranium breadth = greatest breadth of the braincase: Euryon - Euryon (-)
39) Least frontal breadth = least breadth of skull = least breadth of the forehead aboral of the orbits (+)
40) Least breadth between the supraorbital foramina (+)
41) Greatest breadth of skull = greatest breadth across the orbits = greatest frontal breadth* : Ectorbitale - Ectorbitale (+)
42) Least breadth between the orbits: Entorbitale - Entorbitale (+)
43) Facial breadth between the outermost points of the facial crest at the point of intersection of the maxillo-jugal suture with the facial ridge (+, except in old horses, in which the suture may be already obliterated)
44) Facial breadth between the infraorbital foramina (least distance) (-)
45) Greatest breadth of "snout": measured across the outer borders of the alveoli of I^3 (+)
46) Greatest breadth on the curvature of the premaxillae (+)
47) Least breadth in the region of the diastema (+)
48) Greatest palatal breadth: measured across the outer borders of the alveoli (-)
(49) Greatest skull height inclusive of the lower jaws: Gonion ventrale (see below under "Mandible" for point definition) - the highest point of the skull in projection (best measured on a table). Not shown in Fig. 5 (-)
50) Basion height: Basion - the highest point of the skull in projection

*In the literature one often finds this measurement defined as Zygion - Zygion, while Duerst (1926, Fig. 108) has drawn the Ectorbitale and Zygion inaccurately. The most lateral points of the horse skull are the two Ectorbitalia. The Zygion lies rather more basally and less laterally. So the greatest breadth of the skull must be measured between the ectorbital points.

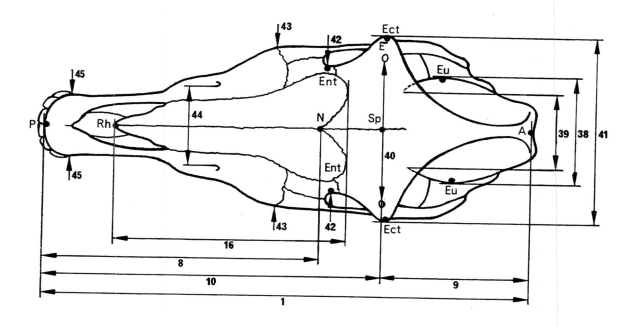

Figure 5a: _Equus_ cranium, dorsal view.

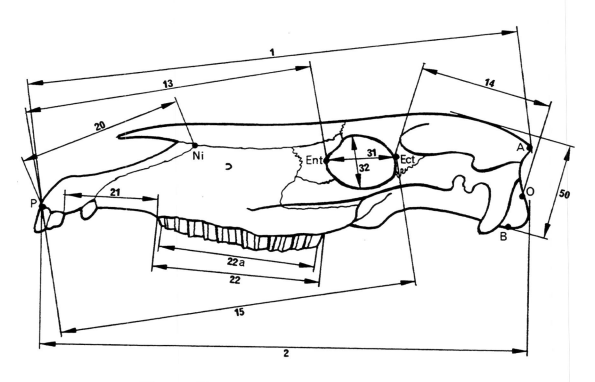

Figure 5b: _Equus_ cranium, left side view.

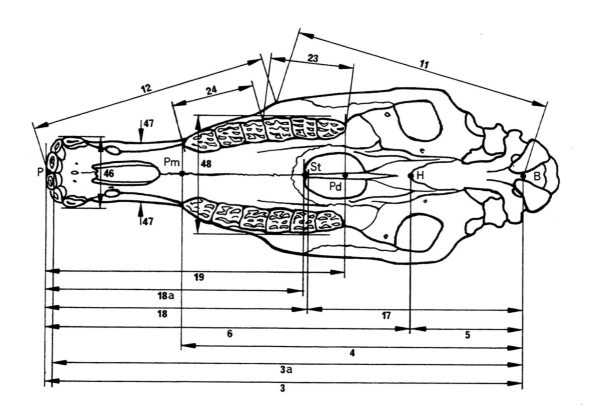

Figure 5c: <u>Equus</u> cranium,
basal view.

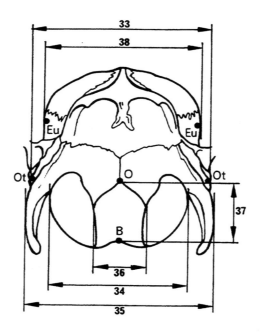

Figure 5d: <u>Equus</u> cranium,
nuchal view.

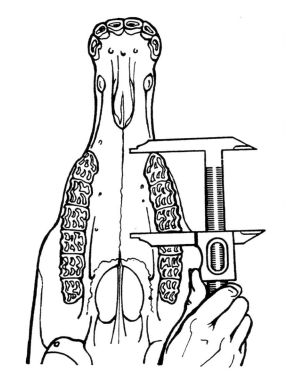

Figure 6a: <u>Equus</u> cranium,
basal view,
showing meas-
urement of
premolar row
(M 24a).

P2   P3–M2   M3

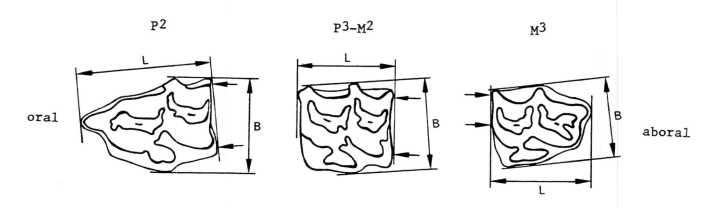

oral   aboral

Figure 6b: Length (L) and breadth (B) at the biting surface of
<u>Equus</u> maxillary teeth. (See M 25-30.)

Measurements of the cranium of Camelus (Fig. 7a,b,c)

1) Profile length – total length: Akrokranion – Prosthion (See definition of point "P" above). (+)
2) Condylobasal length: aboral border of the occipital condyles – Prosthion (+)
3) Basal length: Basion – Prosthion (–)
4) Short skull length: Basion – Premolare (–)
4a) Short skull length: Basion – the median point of intersection of the line joining the oral points of the alveoli of P^3 (+)
5) Lateral neurocranium length: Akrokranion – Ectorbitale on one side (+)
6) Short lateral facial length: Entorbitale – Prosthion (+)
7) Opisthion – Ectorbitale (+)
8) Akrokranion – Infraorbitale (+)
9) Basion – Staphylion (–)
10) Median palatal length: Staphylion – Prosthion (+)
10a) Palatal length: the median point of the line joining the deepest indentation of the choanae – Prosthion (–)
11) Dental length: Postdentale – Prosthion (+)
12) Lateral length of the premaxilla: Nasointermaxillare – Prosthion (+)
13) Length of the cheektooth row, M^3-P^2 (measured along the alveoli) (+)
13a) Length of the cheektooth row, M^3-P^3 (measured along the alveoli) (+)
14) Length of the molar row (measured along the alveoli on the buccal side) (–)
15) Length of the premolar row, P^2-P^4 (measured along the alveoli on the buccal side) (–)
15a) Length of the premolar row, P^3-P^4 (measured along the alveoli) (–)
16) Greatest inner length of the orbit: Ectorbitale – Entorbitale (+)
17) Greatest inner height of the orbit. Measured in the same way as M 16 (+)
18) Greatest mastoid breadth: Otion – Otion (+)
19) Greatest breadth of the occipital condyles (+)
20) Greatest breadth at the bases of the paraoccipital processes (+)
21) Greatest breadth of the foramen magnum (+)
(22) Height of the foramen magnum: Basion – Opisthion. Not shown in Fig. 7 (–)
23) Greatest neurocranium breadth = greatest breadth of the braincase: Euryon – Euryon (–)
24) Least frontal breadth = least breadth of the forehead aboral of the orbits (+)
25) Greatest breadth of skull = greatest breadth across the orbits = greatest frontal breadth: Ectorbitale – Ectorbitale (+)
26) Least breadth between the orbits: Entorbitale – Entorbitale (+)
27) Facial breadth between the infraorbital foramina (least distance) (–)

28) Greatest breadth of the premaxilla: measured in the region of the bony nostril (-)
29) Greatest palatal breadth: measured across the outer borders of the alveoli (-)
30) Basion height: Basion - the highest point of the skull in projection (-)
31) Height of the horizontal part of the maxilla: from the front border of the alveoli of P^3 at right angles to the most dorsal point of the maxilla on one side (-)

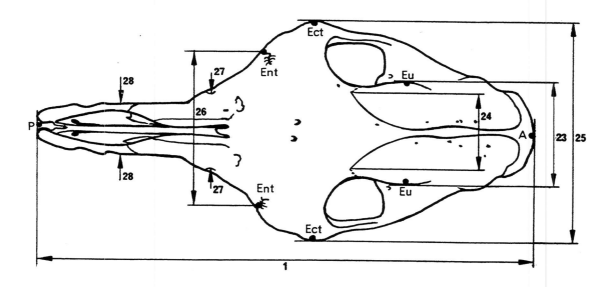

Figure 7a: Camelus cranium, dorsal view.

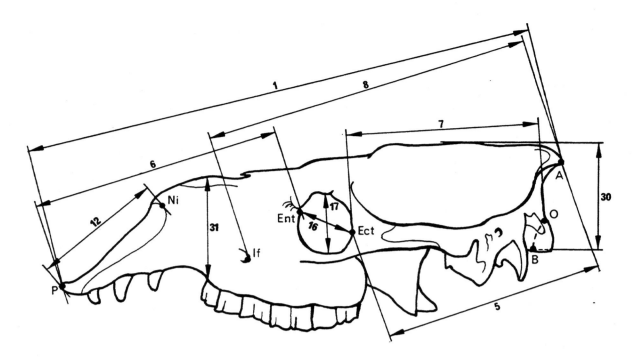

Figure 7b: <u>Camelus</u> cranium, left side view.

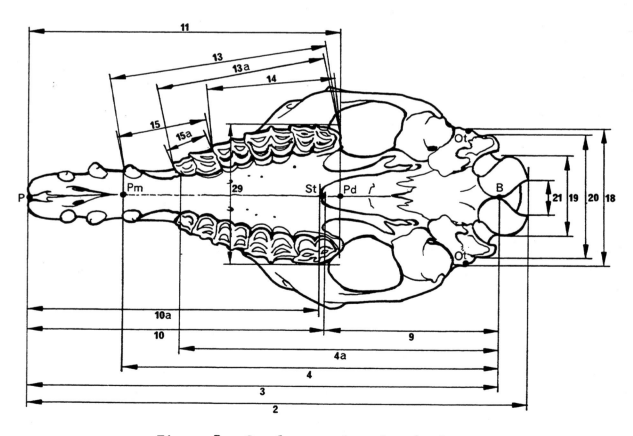

Figure 7c: <u>Camelus</u> cranium, basal view.

Measurements of the cranium of Bos (Fig. 8a,b,c,d)

1) Profile length = total length: Akrokranion - Prosthion (See definition of point "P" above) (+)
2) Condylobasal length: aboral border of the occipital condyles - Prosthion (+)
3) Basal length: Basion - Prosthion (+)
4) Short skull length: Basion - Premolare (+)
5) Premolare - Prosthion (+)
6) Neurocranium length: Basion - Nasion. Can be taken only with curved callipers (-)
7) Viscerocranium length: Nasion - Prosthion (+)
8) Median frontal length: Akrokranion - Nasion (+)
9) Greatest frontal length: Akrokranion - the median point of intersection of the line joining the oral points of the frontals (+)
10) Short upper cranium length: Akrokranion - Rhinion (+)
11) Akrokranion - Infraorbitale of one side (+)
12) Greatest length of the nasals: Nasion - Rhinion (+)
13) From the aboral border of one occipital condyle to the Entorbitale of the same side (+)
14) Lateral facial length: Ectorbitale - Prosthion (+)
15) From the aboral border of one occipital condyle to the Infraorbitale of the same side (+)
16) Infraorbitale - Prosthion (-)
17) Dental length: Postdentale - Prosthion (+)
18) Oral palatal length: Palatinoorale - Prosthion (-)
19) Lateral length of the premaxilla: Nasointermaxillare - Prosthion (+)
20) Length of the cheektooth row (measured along the alveoli) (+)
21) Length of the molar row (measured along the alveoli on the buccal side) (-)
22) Length of the premolar row (measured along the alveoli on the buccal side) (-)
23) Greatest inner length of the orbit: Ectorbitale - Entorbitale (+)
24) Greatest inner height of the orbit. Measured in the same way as M 23 (+)
25) Greatest mastoid breadth: Otion - Otion (+)
26) Greatest breadth of the occipital condyles (+)
27) Greatest breadth at the bases of the paraoccipital processes (+)
28) Greatest breadth of the foramen magnum (+)
29) Height of the foramen magnum: Basion - Opisthion (-)
30) Least occipital breadth: the distance between the most medial points of the aboral borders of the temporal grooves (+)
31) Least breadth between the bases of the horncores (-)
32) Least frontal breadth: breadth of the narrowest part of the frontal aboral of the orbits (+)
33) Greatest breadth across the orbits = greatest frontal breadth = greatest breadth of skull: Ectorbitale - Ectorbitale (+)
34) Least breadth between the orbits: Entorbitale - Entorbitale (+)
35) Facial breadth: across the facial tuberosities (+)
36) Greatest breadth across the nasals (+)
37) Breadth across the premaxillae on the oral protuberances (+)

38) Greatest palatal breadth: measured across the outer borders of the alveoli (-)

39) Least inner height of the temporal groove, roughly from the middle of one bone edge to the other (-)

40) Greatest height of the occipital region: Basion - highest point of the intercornual ridge in the median plane (+)

41) Least height of the occipital region: Opisthion - highest point of the intercornual ridge in the median plane (+)

42) Least distance between the horncore tips (+)

42a) Distance between the horncore tips, measured round the curve with a tape measure (-)

43) Greatest tangential distance between the outer curves of the horncores (+)

Note: Measurements 44-46 are taken exactly on the ring of bony nodules.

(44) Horncore basal circumference. Not shown in Fig. 8 (+)

45) Greatest (oro-aboral) diameter of the horncore base (+)

46) Least (dorso-basal) diameter of the horncore base (+)

47) Length of the outer curvature of the horncore (tape measure) (-)

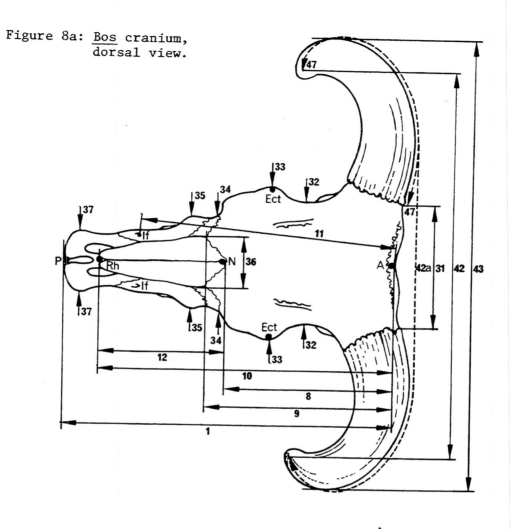

Figure 8a: <u>Bos</u> cranium,
dorsal view.

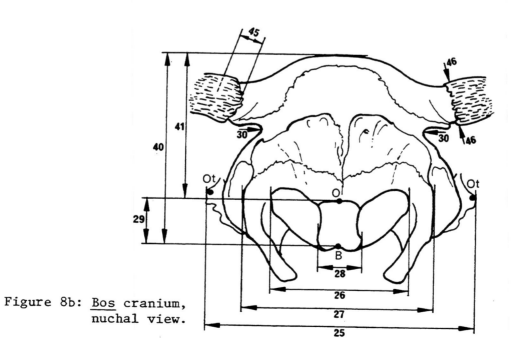

Figure 8b: <u>Bos</u> cranium,
nuchal view.

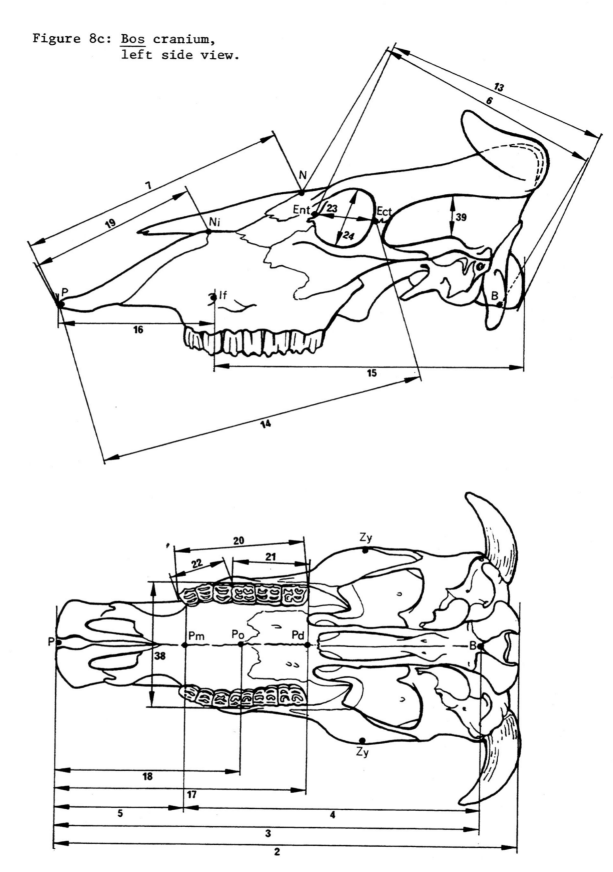

Figure 8c: <u>Bos</u> cranium,
left side view.

Figure 8d: <u>Bos</u> cranium,
basal view.

Measurements of the cranium of Ovis and Capra (Figs. 9a,b,c,d and 10)

1) Profile length: Akrokranion - Prosthion (See definition of Point "P" above) (+)
2) Condylobasal length: aboral border of occipital condyles - Prosthion (+)
3) Basal length: Basion - Prosthion (+)
4) Short skull length: Basion - Premolare (+)
5) Premolare - Prosthion (+)
6) Neurocranium length: Basion - Nasion. Can be taken only with curved callipers (+)
7) Viscerocranium length: Nasion - Prosthion (+)
8) Median frontal length: Akrokranion - Nasion (+)
9) Akrokranion - Bregma (+)
10) Frontal length: Bregma - Nasion (+)
11) Upper neurocranium length: Akrokranion - Supraorbitale (+)
12) Facial length: Supraorbitale - Prosthion
13) Akrokranion - Infraorbitale of one side (+)
14) Greatest length of the lacrimal: most lateral point of the lacrimal - the most oral point of the lacrimo-maxillary suture (+)
15) Greatest length of the nasals: Nasion - Rhinion
16) Short lateral facial length: Entorbitale - Prosthion (+)
17) From the aboral border of one occipital condyle to the Infraorbitale of the same side (+)
18) Dental length: Postdentale - Prosthion (-)
19) Oral palatal length: Palatinoorale - Prosthion (-)
20) Lateral length of the premaxilla: Nasointermaxillare - Prosthion (+)
21) Length of the cheektooth row (measured along the alveoli) (+)
22) Length of the molar row (measured along the alveoli on the buccal side) (-)
23) Length of the premolar row (measured along the alveoli on the buccal side) (-)
24) Greatest inner length of the orbit: Ectorbitale - Entorbitale (+)
25) Greatest inner height of the orbit. Measured in the same way as M 24 (+)
26) Greatest mastoid breadth: Otion - Otion (+)
27) Greatest breadth of the occipital condyles (+)
28) Greatest breadth at the bases of the paraoccipital processes (+)
29) Greatest breadth of the foramen magnum (+)
30) Height of the foramen magnum: Basion - Opisthion (-)
31) Least breadth of parietal = least breadth between the temporal lines (+)
32) Greatest breadth between the lateral borders of the horncore bases (+)
33) Greatest neurocranium breadth = greatest breadth of the braincase: Euryon - Euryon (-)
34) Greatest breadth across the orbits = greatest frontal breadth = greatest breadth of skull: Ectorbitale - Ectorbitale (+)
35) Least breadth between the orbits: Entorbitale - Entorbitale (-)
36) Facial breadth: breadth across the facial tuberosities (+)
37) Greatest breadth across the nasals (+)

Figure 9a: <u>Ovis</u> cranium, dorsal view.

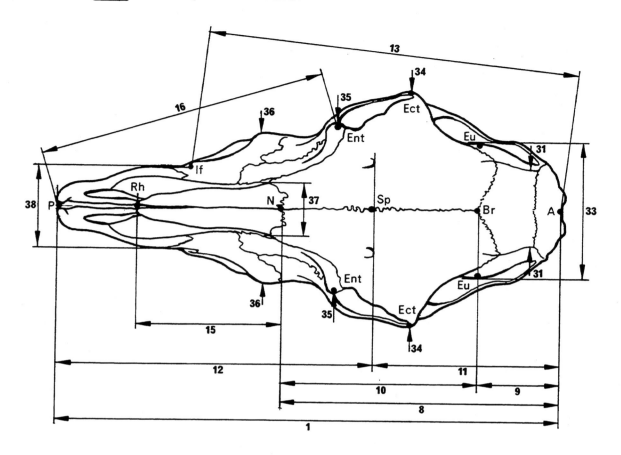

Figure 9b: <u>Ovis</u> cranium, left side view.

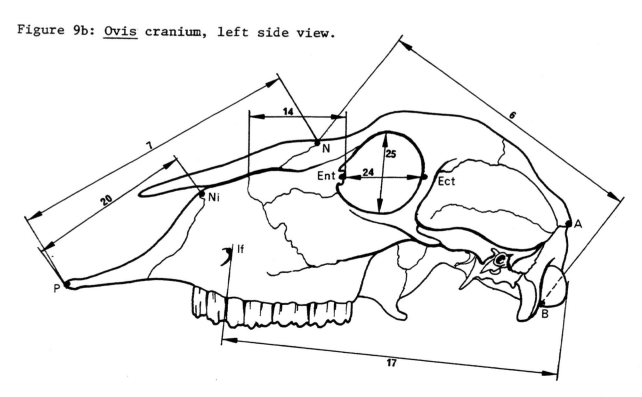

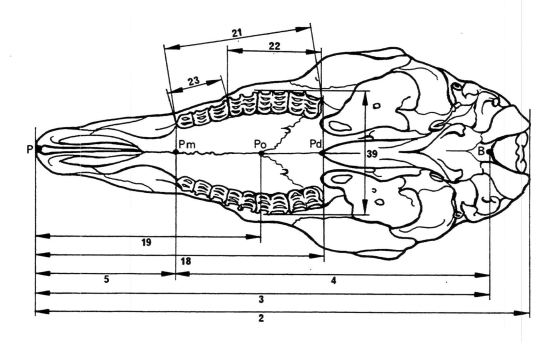

Figure 9c: <u>Ovis</u> cranium, basal view.

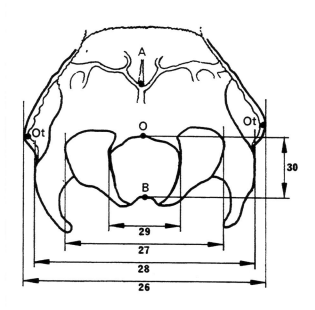

Figure 9d: <u>Ovis</u> cranium, nuchal view.

38) Greatest breadth across the premaxillae (+)
39) Greatest palatal breadth: measured across the outer borders of
    the alveoli (-)
40) Horncore basal circumference
41) Greatest (oro-aboral) diameter of the horncore base (+)
42) Least (latero-medial) diameter of the horncore base (+)
(43) Length of the horncore on the front margin (tape measure). Not
    shown in Fig. 10 (+)

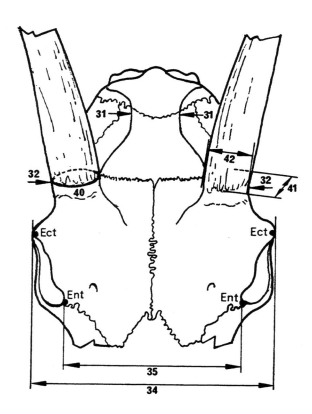

Figure 10: Capra cranium, dorsal view.

Measurements of the cranium of Cervus (Fig. 11a,b,c)

1) Total length = greatest length: Akrokranion - Prosthion (See definition of point "P" above) (+)
2) Condylobasal length: aboral border of the occipital condyles - Prosthion (+)
3) Basal length: Basion - Prosthion (+)
4) Short skull length: Basion - Premolare (+)
5) Premolare - Prosthion (+)
6) Basicranial axis: Basion - Synsphenion (-)
7) Basifacial axis: Synsphenion - Prosthion (-)
8) Neurocranium length: Basion - Nasion. Can be taken only with curved callipers (+)
9) Viscerocranium length: Nasion - Prosthion (+)
10) Median frontal length: Akrokranion - Nasion (+)
11) Lambda - Nasion (+)
12) Lambda - Rhinion (+)
13) Lambda - Prosthion (+)
14) Akrokranion - Infraorbitale of one side (+)
15) Greatest length of the nasals: Nasion - Rhinion (-)
16) Short lateral facial length (="snout" length): Entorbitale of one side - Prosthion (+)
17) Median palatal length: Staphylion - Prosthion (-)
18) Oral palatal length: Palatinoorale - Prosthion (-)
19) Lateral length of the premaxilla: Nasointermaxillare - Prosthion (+)
20) Length of the cheektooth row (measured along the alveoli) (+)
21) Length of the molar row (measured along the alveoli on the buccal side) (-)
22) Length of the premolar row (measured along the alveoli on the buccal side) (-)
23) Greatest inner length of the orbit: Ectorbitale - Entorbitale (+)
24) Greatest inner height of the orbit. Measured in the same way as M 23 (+)
25) Greatest mastoid breadth: Otion - Otion (+)
26) Greatest breadth of the occipital condyles (+)
27) Greatest breadth at the bases of the paraoccipital processes (+)
28) Greatest breadth of the foramen magnum (+)
(29) Height of the foramen magnum: Basion - Opisthion. Not shown in Fig. 11 (-)
(30) Greatest neurocranium breadth = greatest breadth of the braincase: Euryon - Euryon. Not shown in Fig. 11 (-)
31) Least frontal breadth = least breadth of the forehead aboral of the orbits (+)
32) Greatest breadth across the orbits = greatest frontal breadth = nearly greatest breadth of skull: Ectorbitale - Ectorbitale (+)
33) Least breadth between the orbits: Entorbitale - Entorbitale (+)
34) Zygomatic breadth: Zygion - Zygion (+)
35) Greatest breadth across the nasals (-)
36) Greatest breadth across the premaxillae (+)
37) Greatest palatal breadth: measured across the outer borders of the alveoli (-)

38) Basion - the highest point of the superior nuchal crest (+)
39) Circumference of the burr. The tape measure should be placed
    exactly on the bony nodules of the burr (-)
40) Proximal circumference of the burr = circumference of the distal
    end of the pedicel (+)
41) Distal circumference of the burr (+)
(42) Neurocranium capacity (cc., see M 42 of Canis)

Note: For the measurement of antlers (and horncores) refer to specialized
works such as Haltenorth and Trense 1956, pp. 55 ff.

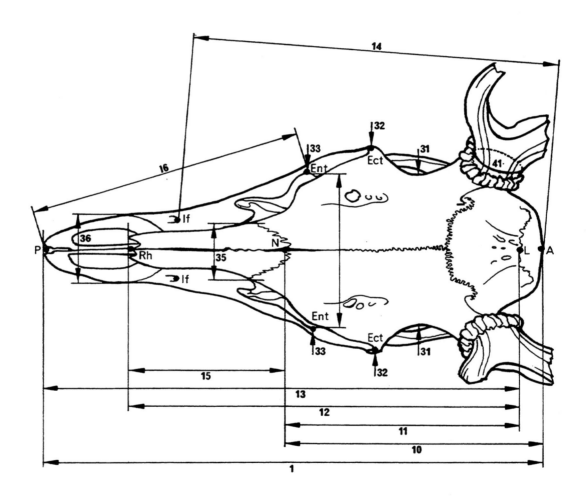

Figure 11a: Cervus cranium, dorsal view.

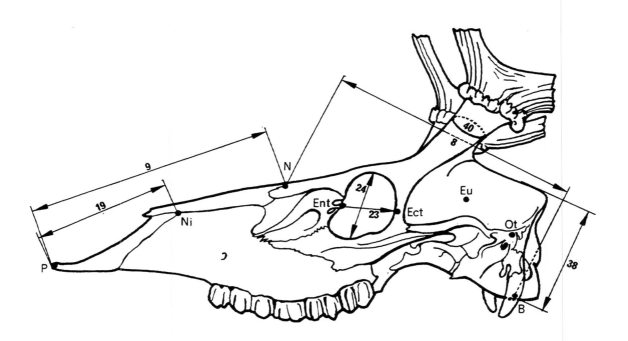

Figure 11b: _Cervus_ cranium, left side view.

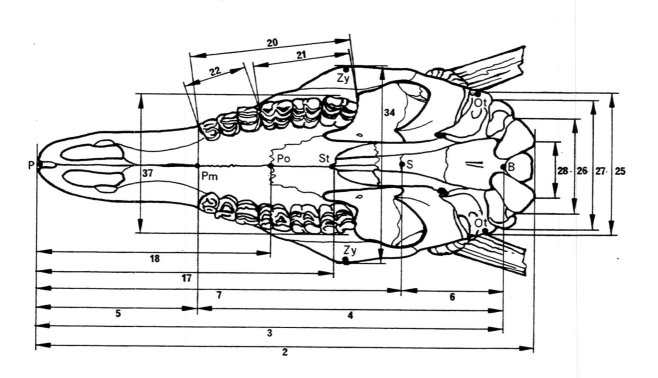

Figure 11c: _Cervus_ cranium, basal view.

Measurements of the cranium of Sus (Figs. 12a,b,c,d,e,f and 13)

1) Profile length: Akrokranion - Prosthion (See definition of point "P" above) (+)
1a) Opisthokranion - Prosthion (See discussion under "Skull" above.) The opisthokranion lies in space and is best established when one point of the slide gauge touches the two most aboral points of the linea nuchalis superior (+)
2) Condylobasal length: aboral border of the occipital condyles - Prosthion (+)
3) Basal length: Basion - Prosthion (+)
4) Short skull length: Basion - Premolare (+)
5) Premolare - Prosthion (+)
6) Basicranial axis: Basion - Hormion (-)
7) Basifacial axis: Hormion - Prosthion (-)
8) Neurocranium length: Basion - Nasion. Can be taken only with curved callipers (+)
9) Median frontal length: Akrokranion - Nasion (+)
10) Viscerocranium length: Nasion - Prosthion (+)
11) Upper neurocranium length: Akrokranion - Supraorbitale (+)
12) Facial length: Supraorbitale - Prosthion (+)
13) Parietal length: Akrokranion - Bregma (+)
14) Frontal length: Bregma - Nasion (+)
Note: In very old pigs the parieto-frontal suture is obliterated and the Bregma is no longer visible.
15) Greatest length of the nasals: Nasion - Rhinion (+)
15a) Short nasal length: Nasion - median point of intersection of the line joining the most aboral points of the naso-maxillary suture (-)
16) Basion - Staphylion (-)
17) Median palatal length: Staphylion - Prosthion (+)
18) Dental length: Postdentale - Prosthion (+)
19) Entorbitale - Infraorbitale (-)
20) Infraorbitale - Prosthion (-)
21) Upper length of the lacrimal: aboral-dorsal point of the lacrimal on the orbital rim - the most oral point of the fronto-lacrimal suture (see Fig. 12b) (-)
22) Height of the lacrimal. Formerly called "breadth" (see definitions of linear measurements above). Measured from the most dorsal point where the lacrimal, jugal, and maxilla meet (-)
23) Lateral length of the premaxilla: Nasointermaxillare - Prosthion (+)
24) Greatest inner length of the orbit: Ectorbitale - Entorbitale (-)
25) Length from the aboral border of the alveolus of M^3 - aboral border of the alveolus of C (+)
26) Length from the oral border of the alveolus of P^1 - aboral border of the alveolus of I^3 (+)
27) Length of the cheektooth row (measured along the alveoli) (+)
27a) Length of the cheektooth row, M^3-P^2 (measured along the alveoli) (-)

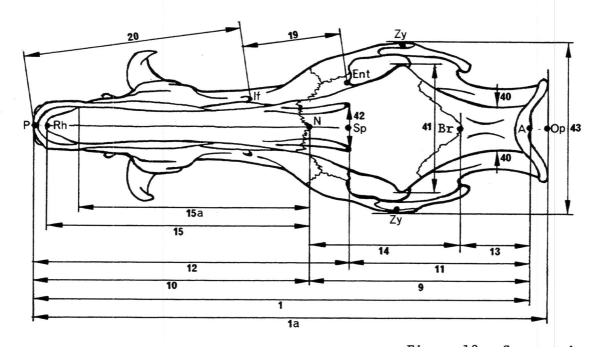

Figure 12a: <u>Sus</u> cranium, dorsal view.

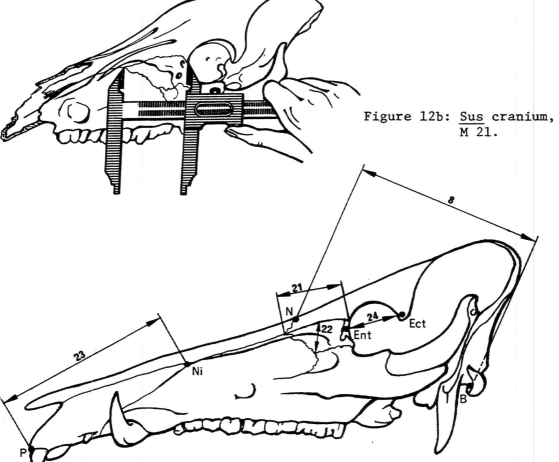

Figure 12b: <u>Sus</u> cranium, M 21.

Figure 12c: <u>Sus</u> cranium, left side view.

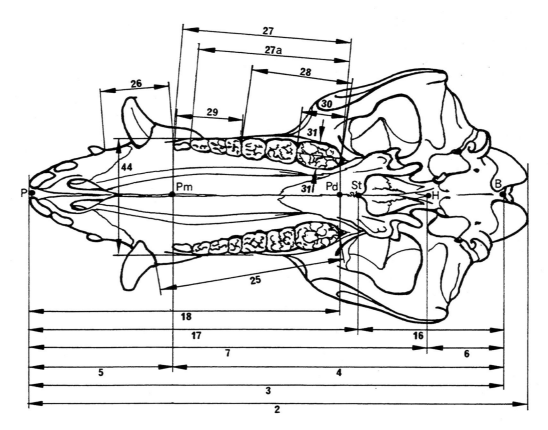

Figure 12d: *Sus* cranium, basal view.

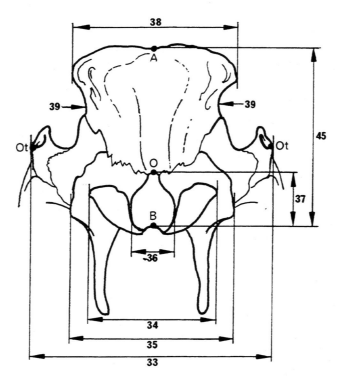

Figure 12e: *Sus* cranium, nuchal view.

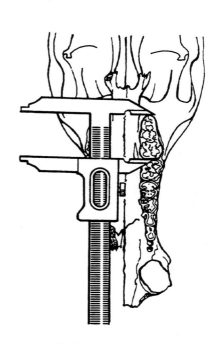

Figure 12f: *Sus* cranium, M 30.

28) Length of the molar row (measured along the alveoli on the buccal side) (−)

29) Length of the premolar row (measured along the alveoli on the buccal side) (−)

(29a) Length of the premolar row, P^2-P^4 (measured along the alveoli on the buccal side). Not shown in Fig. 12 (−)

30) Length of M^3 measured near the base of the crown (Fig. 12f) (−)

31) Breadth of M^3 measured near the base of the crown (−)

(32) Greatest diameter of the canine alveolus. Not shown in Fig. 12 female (+), male (−)

33) Greatest mastoid breadth = breadth across the openings of the external auditory meatus: Otion − Otion (+)

34) Greatest breadth of the occipital condyles (+)

35) Greatest breadth at the bases of the paraoccipital processes (+)

36) Greatest breadth of the foramen magnum (+)

37) Height of the foramen magnum: Basion − Opisthion (−)

38) Greatest breadth of the squamous part of the occipital bone (+)

39) Least breadth of the squamous part of the occipital bone = breadth at the narrowest points of the lineae nuchales laterales (+)

40) Least breadth of the parietal = least breadth between the temporal lines (+)

41) Greatest frontal breadth = greatest breadth across the supraorbital processes: Ectorbitale − Ectorbitale (+)

42) Least breadth between the supraorbital foramina (+)

43) Zygomatic breadth = greatest breadth of skull: Zygion − Zygion (+)

44) Greatest palatal breadth: measured across the outer borders of the alveoli (−)

45) Height of the occipital region: Basion − Akrokranion (+)

46) Angle between the lines of measurements nos. 3 and 45

47) Angle between the lines of measurements nos. 3 and 1

48) Angle between the lines of measurements nos. 1 and 45

Note: These three angles can be graphically established (following Reitsma 1935, p. 15 and Figs. 40, 89, and 90). One marks off the basal length on a straight line with a pair of compasses, and then still using compasses one marks off the other two lines in the same proportions, as shown in Figure 13. The angles can then be read off by using a protractor.

Figure 13: Sus cranium, calculation of M 46, 47, 48.
Example: Profile length: 268 mm.
Basal length: 250 mm.
Height of occipital region: 89 mm.

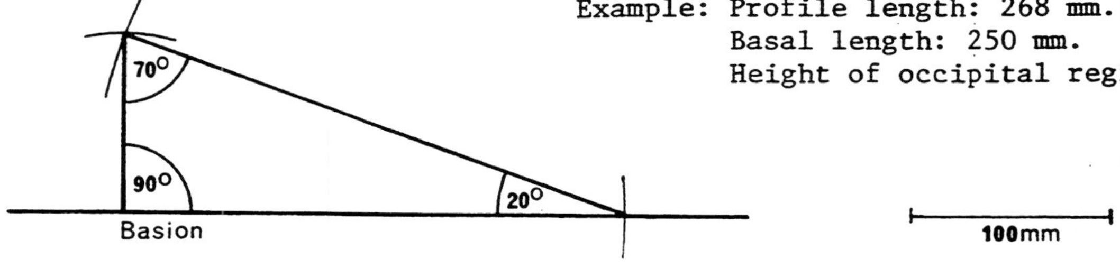

Measurements of the cranium of <u>Canis</u> (Figs. 14a,b,c,d and 15a,b,c)

1) Total length: Akrokranion - Prosthion (+)
2) Condylobasal length: aboral border of the occipital condyles - Prosthion (+)
3) Basal length: Basion - Prosthion (+)
4) Basicranial axis: Basion - Synsphenion (= Intersphenoid suture) (+)
5) Basifacial axis: Synsphenion - Prosthion (+)
(6) Neurocranium length: Basion - Nasion. Not shown in Fig. 14. Can be taken only with curved callipers (+)
7) Upper neurocranium length: Akrokranion - Frontal midpoint (+)
8) Viscerocranium length: Nasion - Prosthion (+)
9) Facial length: Frontal midpoint - Prosthion (+)
10) Greatest length of the nasals: Nasion - Rhinion (-)
11) Length of braincase (following Wagner 1930, p. 13). This measurement can be taken only when the cribriform plate is preserved. One inserts a thin ruler through the foramen magnum; the front end must reach the cribriform plate and the measurement is read off against the Basion (-)
12) "Snout" length: oral border of the orbits (median) - Prosthion (+)
13) Median palatal length: Staphylion - Prosthion (+)
13a) Palatal length: the median point of intersection of the line joining the deepest indentations of the Choanae - Prosthion (-)
14) Length of the horizontal part of the palatine: Staphylion - Palatinoorale (+)
14a) Length of the horizontal part of the palatine corresponding to M 13a (-)
15)* Length of cheektooth row (measured along the alveoli on the buccal side) (-)
16) Length of the molar row (measured along the alveoli on the buccal side) (-)
17) Length of the premolar row (measured along the alveoli on the buccal side) (-)
18) Length of the carnassial, measured at the cingulum (Fig. 15a) (+)
18a) Greatest breadth of the carnassial (Fig. 15a) (-) Until now the breadth of the carnassial has been measured without the medial projection. Because this dimension is difficult to measure exactly I propose to leave it out and to measure only the greatest breadth.
(19) Length of the carnassial alveolus. Not shown in Fig. 14 (-)
20) Length and breadth of M^1, measured at the cingulum (see Fig. 15b) (-)
21) Length and breadth of M^2, measured at the cingulum (see Fig. 15c) (-)

*For wild canids another length measurement is also important:
(15a) Aboral border of the alveolus of M^2 - oral border of the alveolus of C. Not shown in Fig. 14.

22) Greatest diameter of the auditory bulla (following Wagner 1930, p. 21): from the most aboral point of the bulla on the suture with the paraoccipital process up to the external carotid foramen (-)
23) Greatest mastoid breadth = greatest breadth of the occipital triangle: Otion - Otion (+)
24) Breadth dorsal to the external auditory meatus (+)
25) Greatest breadth of the occipital condyles (+)
26) Greatest breadth of the bases of the paraoccipital processes (+)
27) Greatest breadth of the foramen magnum (-)
28) Height of the foramen magnum: Basion - Opisthion (-)
29) Greatest neurocranium breadth = greatest breadth of the braincase: Euryon - Euryon (-)
30) Zygomatic breadth: Zygion - Zygion (+)
31) Least breadth of skull = least breadth aboral of the supraorbital processes = breadth at the postorbital constriction* (+)
32) Frontal breadth: Ectorbitale - Ectorbitale (+)
33) Least breadth between the orbits: Entorbitale - Entorbitale (+)
34) Greatest palatal breadth: measured across the outer borders of the alveoli (-)
35) Least palatal breadth: measured behind the canines (-)
36) Breadth at the canine alveoli (+)
37) Greatest inner height of the orbit (+)
38) Skull height (following Wagner 1930, p. 19). The two pointers of the slide gauge are placed basally on the basis of the skull (on the basioccipital) and dorsally on the highest elevation of the sagittal crest (+)
39) Skull height without the sagittal crest (following Wagner 1930, pp.19 ff.) the slide gauge is placed in the same position as for M 38 with the difference that the upper pointer is placed beside the sagittal crest on the highest point of the braincase (-)
40) Height of the occipital triangle: Akrokranion - Basion (-)
(41) Height (length) of the canine, measured in a straight line from point to point. This measurement is only possible if the tooth can be removed from the jaw (+)
(42) Neurocranium capacity = capacity of the braincase (cc). This can only be measured when the ethmoid is preserved. The foramina of the braincase are stopped up with wadding; when it is completely free of dirt and earth the braincase is filled with millet seeds and shaken repeatedly to remove air pockets. Finally, the seeds are tipped into a measuring beaker and their volume is read off (+)

*According to Duerst 1926, p. 238 = Frontostenion - Frontostenion

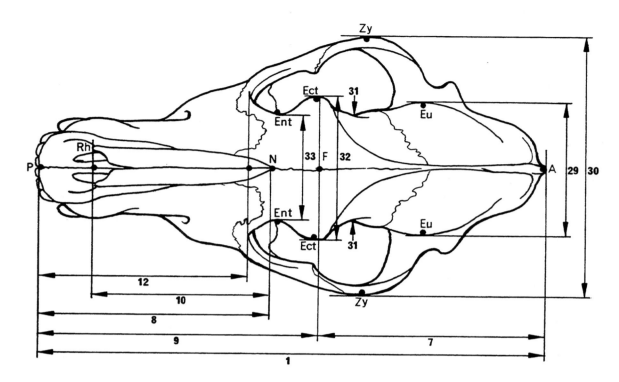

Figure 14a: Canis cranium, dorsal view.

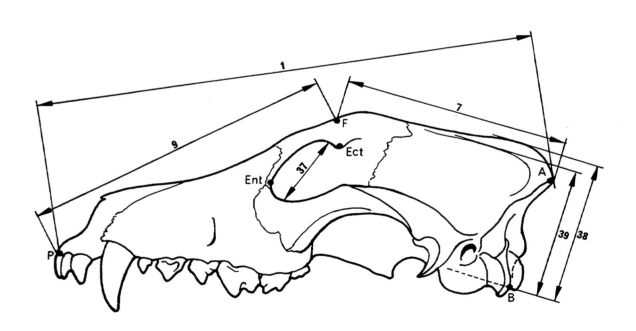

Figure 14b: Canis cranium, left side view.

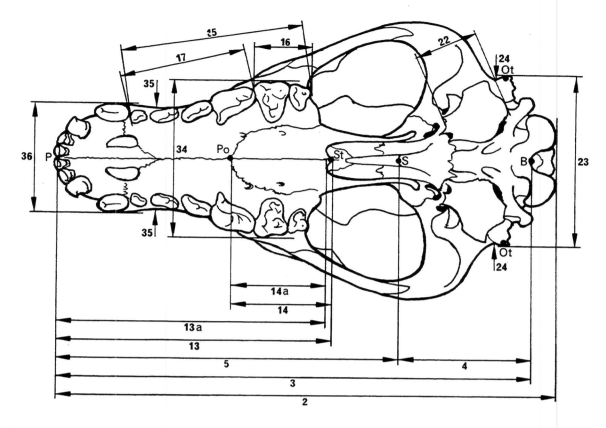

Figure 14c: _Canis_ cranium, basal view.

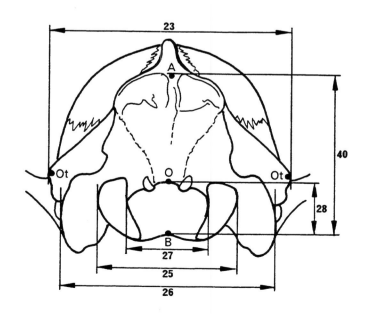

Figure 14d: _Canis_ cranium, nuchal view.

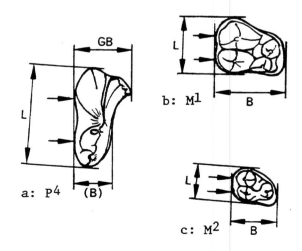

Figure 15a-c:
Canis maxillary teeth,
Length (L) and breadth (B)
M 18,18a,20,21

Measurements of the cranium of Ursus (Fig. 16a,b,c)

Because the skull of the bear is very similar in form to that of the dog, one can use the same dimensions for its measurement. One has to leave out measurements no. 13a and 14a because the indentation of the edges of the Choanae is much weaker in bears. Also it is unusual for the neurocranium capacity of bears to be measured.

Additionally, the following toothrow measurement should be taken:

Length from P^4 - M^2 (measured along the alveoli on the buccal side) (-)

The taking of length and breadth measurements of single teeth (P^4-M^2) should be done as depicted in Figure 16a-c. Single teeth can be measured properly only when they are removed from the alveoli.

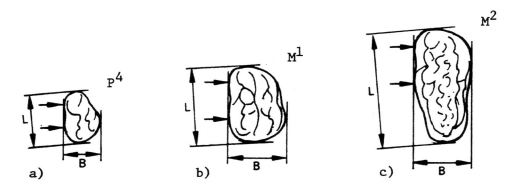

Figure 16a-c: <u>Ursus</u> maxillary teeth, length (L) and breadth (B)

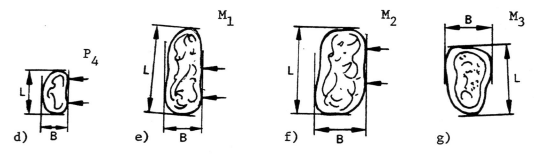

Figure 16d-g: <u>Ursus</u> mandibular teeth, length (L) and breadth (B)
(See below, page 62.)

Measurements of the cranium of Felis (Fig. 17a,b,c)

1) Total length: Akrokranion – Prosthion (+)
2) Condylobasal length: aboral border of the occipital condyles – Prosthion (+)
3) Basal length: Basion – Prosthion (+)
4) Basicranial axis: Basion – Synsphenion (= Interspenoid suture) (+)
5) Basifacial axis: Synsphenion – Prosthion (+)
6) Neurocranium length: Basion – Nasion. Can be taken only with curved callipers (+)
7) Upper neurocranium length: Akrokranion – Frontal midpoint (+)
8) Viscerocranium length: Nasion – Prosthion (+)
9) Facial length: Frontal midpoint – Prosthion (+)
10) Lateral length of "snout": oral border of the orbit of one side – Prosthion (+)
11) Median palatal length: Staphylion – Prosthion (+)
11a) Palatal length: the median point of intersection of the line joining the deepest indentations of the Choanae – Prosthion (–)
12) Length of the cheektooth row (measured along the alveoli on the buccal side) (–)
13) Length of the premolar row (measured along the alveoli on the buccal side) (–)
14) Length of P^4. As in the dog taken from the buccal part of the cingulum (–)
(15) Length of the carnassial alveolus. Not shown in Fig. 17 (+)
16) Greatest diameter of the auditory bulla: from the most aborolateral point to the most oromedial point (–)
17) Least diameter of the auditory bulla: from the middle of the opening of the external acoustic meatus up to the most medial protrusion of the bulla on the opposite side of the bulla (–)
18) Greatest mastoid breadth = greatest breadth of the occipital triangle: Otion – Otion (+)
19) Greatest breadth of the occipital condyles (+)
20) Greatest breadth of the foramen magnum (+)
21) Height of the foramen magnum: Basion – Opisthion (+)
22) Greatest neurocranium breadth = greatest breadth of braincase: Euryon – Euryon (–)
23) Zygomatic breadth: Zygion – Zygion (+)
24) Frontal breadth: Ectorbitale – Ectorbitale (+)
25) Least breadth between the orbits: Entorbitale – Entorbitale (+)
26) Greatest palatal breadth: measured across the outer borders of the alveoli (–)
27) Breadth at the canine alveoli (+)
28) Least breadth aboral of the supraorbital processes = breadth of the postorbital constriction (+)
29) Facial breadth between the infraorbital foramina (least distance) (+)
30) Greatest inner length of the orbit: Ectorbitale – Entorbitale (+)
31) Greatest inner height of the orbit (+)
32) Height of the occipital triangle: Akrokranion – Basion (–)
(33) Neurocranium capacity = capacity of braincase (cc). Taken in the same way as for the dog M 42 (+)

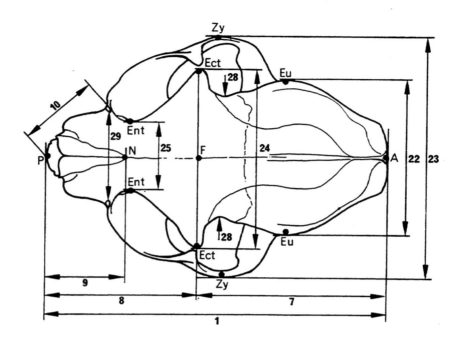

Figure 17a: _Felis_ cranium, dorsal view.

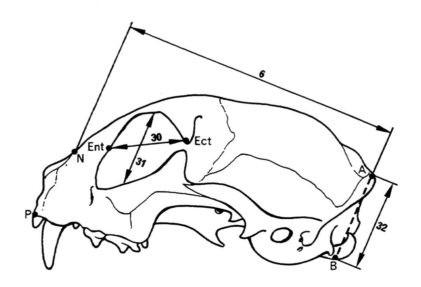

Figure 17b: _Felis_ cranium, left side view.

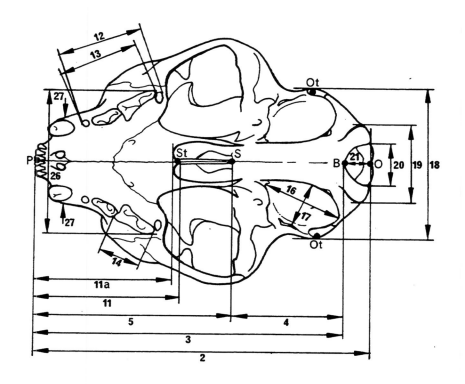

Figure 17c: <u>Felis</u> cranium, basal view.

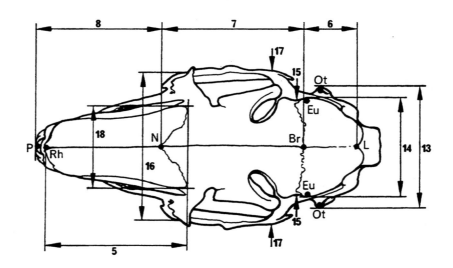

Figure 18a: _Lepus_ cranium, dorsal view.

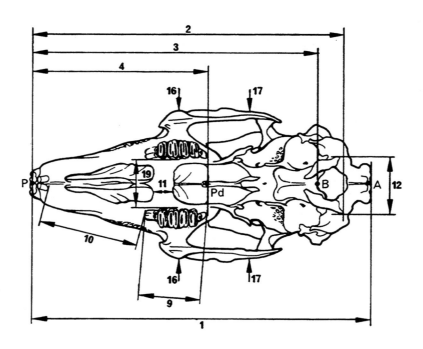

Figure 18b: _Lepus_ cranium, basal view.

Measurements of the cranium of <u>Lepus</u> and <u>Oryctolagus</u> (Fig. 18a,b)

1) Total length: Akrokranion - Prosthion (+)
2) Condylobasal length: aboral border of the occipital condyles - Prosthion (-)
3) Basal length: Basion - Prosthion (+)
4) Dental length: Postdentale - Prosthion (-)
5) Greatest length of the nasals: the median point of intersection of the line joining the aboral borders of the nasals - Rhinion (+)
6) Parietal length: Lambda - Bregma (+)
7) Frontal length: Bregma - Nasion (+)
8) Viscerocranium length: Nasion - Prosthion (+)
9) Length of the cheektooth row (measured along the alveoli on the buccal side) (+)
10) Length of the diastema: the oral border of the alveolus of P^2 - aboral border of the alveolus of I^2 of one side (-)
11) Palatal length (following Hauser 1921, p. 54): the length of the palatal bridge of one side (+)
12) Greatest breadth of the occipital condyles (+)
13) Greatest breadth across the openings of the external acoustic meatus (+)
14) Greatest neurocranium breadth = greatest breadth of the braincase: Euryon - Euryon (-)
15) Breadth of skull (following Hauser 1921, p. 53). The points of the slide gauge are placed in the temporal fossae dorsal of the zygomatic processes of the temporal (+)
16) Oral zygomatic breadth (following Hauser 1921, p. 54): greatest breadth across the oral part of the zygomatic arch (+)
17) Aboral zygomatic breadth (following Hauser 1921, p. 54): greatest breadth across the aboral part of the zygomatic arch (+)
18) Greatest breadth of the nasals
19) Palatal breadth (following Hauser 1921, p. 54): breadth between the inner borders of the alveoli of the second cheekteeth (-)

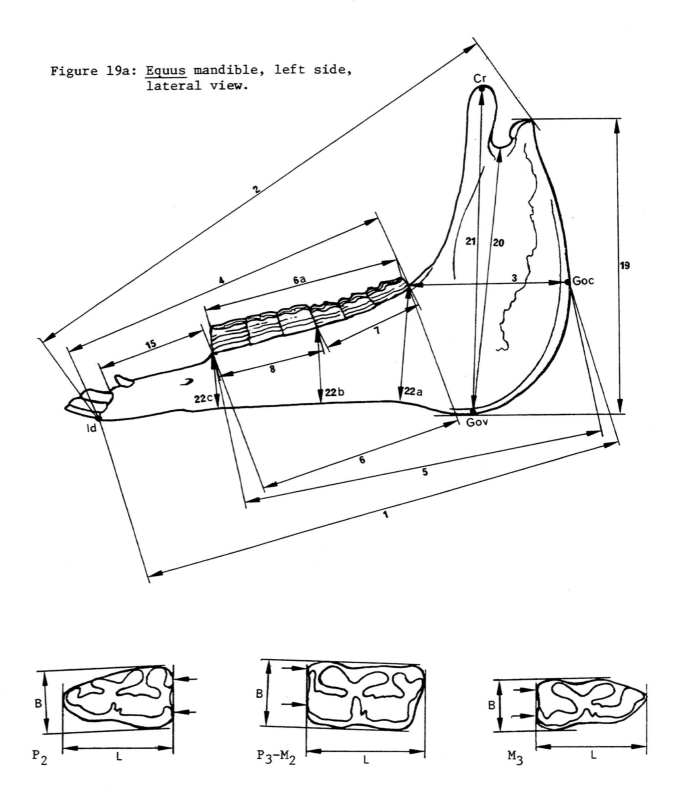

Figure 19a: _Equus_ mandible, left side, lateral view.

Figure 19b: _Equus_ mandibular teeth, length (L) and breadth (B) at the biting surface (see M 9,10,11,12,13,14.)

MANDIBLE

The most important measuring points of the mandible (according to Duerst 1926, pp. 243 ff.) are the following:

Cr – Coronion – the highest point of the coronoid process
Goc – Gonion caudale – the most aboral point of the angle of mandible
Gol – Gonion laterale – the most lateral point of the angle
Gov – Gonion ventrale – the most basal point of the angle
Id – Infradentale – the most prominent median point at the oral border
      of the alveoli of the incisors (corresponds to the Prosthion of
      maxilla).

Note that all length and height measurements for the mandible refer to only one-half of the jaw.

Measurements of the mandible of Equus (Fig. 19a,b)

1) Length from the angle: Gonion caudale – Infradentale (+)
2) Length from the condyle: aboral border of the condyle process – Infradentale (+)
3) Length: Gonion caudale – aboral border of the alveolus of M_3 (–)
4) Length of the horizontal ramus: aboral border of the alveolus of M_3 – Infradentale (+)
5) Length: Gonion caudale – oral border of the alveolus of P_2 (+)
6) Length of the cheektooth row, measured along the alveoli on the buccal side (+)
6a) Length of the cheektooth row, measured near the biting surface (+)
7) Length of the molar row, measured along the alveoli on the buccal side (–)
7a) Length of the molar row, measured near the biting surface as with the maxilla (–)
8) Length of the premolar row, measured along the alveoli on the buccal side (–)
8a) Length of the premolar row, measured near the biting surface as with the maxilla (Fig. 6a) (–)
9) Length and breadth of P_2 (near the biting surface) (–) ⎫
10) Length and breadth of P_3 (near the biting surface) (–) ⎪
11) Length and breadth of P_4 (near the biting surface) (–) ⎬ Fig. 19b
12) Length and breadth of M_1 (near the biting surface) (–) ⎪
13) Length and breadth of M_2 (near the biting surface) (–) ⎪
14) Length and breadth of M_3 (near the biting surface) (–) ⎭
15) Length of the diastema: oral border of the alveolus of P_2 – aboral border of the alveolus of I_3 (+)

(16)   Greatest breadth across the curvature of incisors, measured at the outer borders of the alveoli of I_3. Not shown in Fig. 19a (+)

(17)   Greatest breadth across the curvature of incisors, measured near the biting surface of the I_3. Not shown in Fig. 19a (+)

(18)   Smallest breadth of the two halves in the region of the diastema. Not shown in Fig. 19a (+)

19)   Aboral height of the vertical ramus: Gonion ventrale – highest point of the condyle process. Usually measured in projection. Best measured on the table or by placing one arm of the slide gauge along the basal border of the mandible and measuring the distance in projection (see Duerst 1926, p. 333) (–)

20)   Middle height of the vertical ramus: Gonion ventrale – deepest point of the mandibular notch. Not to be measured in projection but directly from the Gonion ventrale (see Duerst 1926, p. 333) (+)

21)   Oral height of the vertical ramus: Gonion ventrale – Coronion. Not to be measured in projection, but like measurement no. 20 directly from the Gonion ventrale (see Duerst 1926, p. 334) (+)

22a)   Height of the mandible behind M_3 from the most aboral point of the alveolus (–)

22b)   Height of the mandible in front of M_1. Measured at right angles to the basal border (–)

22c)   Height of the mandible in front of P_2. Measured at right angles to the basal border (–)

Note: The height measurements can be taken on the lingual or buccal side, wherever they are easier to take. Indicate from which side the measurements have been made.

(23)   Breadth of the two halves between the most lateral points of the two angles = Gonion laterale – Gonion laterale. Not shown in Fig. 19a (+)

(24)   Breadth of the two halves between the condyle processes: measured between the most lateral points of the two condyle processes. Not shown in Fig. 19a (+)

(25)   Breadth of the two halves between the coronoid processes: measured between the most lateral points of the two coronoid processes. Not shown in Fig. 19a (–)

Measurements of the mandible of <u>Camelus</u> *(Fig. 20)*

1)-4)   Same as <u>Equus</u> measurements.
5)   Gonion caudale - oral border of the alveolus of P_3 (+)
6)   Length of the cheektooth row, M_3-P_3, measured along the alveoli on the buccal side (+)
6a)   Length of the cheektooth row, M_3-P_4, measured along the alveoli on the buccal side (+)
7)   Length of the molar row, measured along the alveoli on the buccal side (−)
8)   Length and breadth of M_3, measured near the biting surface (Fig. 21b) (−)
9)   Length of the diastema between P_4 and P_3: oral border of the alveolus of P_4 – aboral border of the alveolus of P_3 (+)
10)   Aboral height of the vertical ramus: Gonion ventrale – highest point of the condyle process (see <u>Equus</u> M 19) (+)
11)   Middle height of the vertical ramus: Gonion ventrale – deepest point of the mandibular notch (see <u>Equus</u> M 20) (+)
12)   Oral height of the vertical ramus: Gonion ventrale – Coronion (see <u>Equus</u> M 21) (+)
13)   Height of the mandible behind M_3, from the most aboral point of the alveolus. Measured at right angles to the basal border (−)

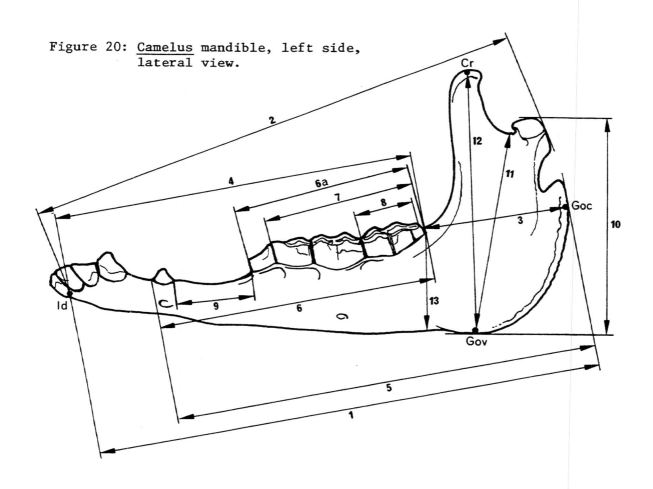

Figure 20: <u>Camelus</u> mandible, left side, lateral view.

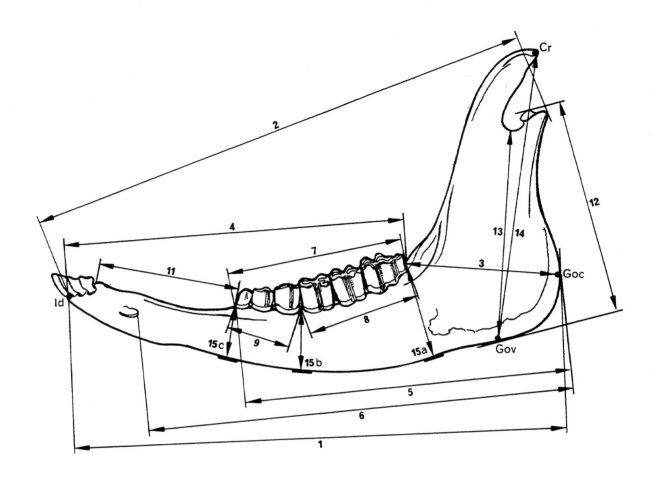

Figure 21a: <u>Bos</u> mandible, left side, lateral view.

Figure 21b: <u>Bos</u> M_3

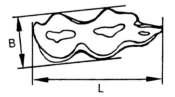

Length (L) and breadth (B)
at the biting surface.
(see M 10)

Measurements of the mandible of Ruminantia with the exception of Camelus
   (Fig. 21a,b)

1)-5)   Same as Equus measurements
   6)   Length: Gonion caudale - the most aboral indentation of the mental
         foramen (+)
   7)   Length of the cheektooth row, measured along the alveoli on the
         buccal side (+)
   8)   Length of the molar row, measured along the alveoli on the buccal
         side (-)
   9)   Length of the premolar row, measured along the alveoli on the
         buccal side (-)
  10)   Length and breadth of M_3, measured near the biting surface
         (Fig. 21b) (-)
  11)   Length of the diastema: oral border of the alveolus of P_2 - aboral
         border of the alveolus of $I_4(=C)$ (+)
  12)   Aboral height of the vertical ramus: Gonion ventrale - highest
         point of the condyle process (see Equus M 19) (+)
  13)   Middle height of the vertical ramus: Gonion ventrale - deepest
         point of the mandibular notch (see Equus M 20) (+)
  14)   Oral height of the vertical ramus: Gonion ventrale - Coronion
         (see Equus M 21) (+)
 15a)   Height of the mandible behind M_3 from the most aboral point of
         the alveolus on the buccal side (-)
 15b)   Height of the mandible in front of M_1 (see note after Equus M 22c)
         (-)
 15c)   Height of the mandible in front of P_2 (see note after Equus M 22c)
         (-)

Figure 22a: <u>Sus</u> M$_3$

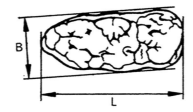

Length (L) and breadth (B)
near the base of the crown.
(see M 10)

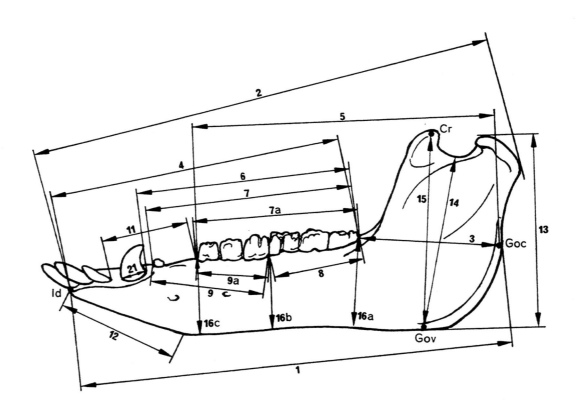

Figure 22b: <u>Sus</u> mandible, left side, lateral view.

Measurements of the mandible of Sus (Fig. 22a,b)

1)-5)   Same as Equus measurements

6)   Length: aboral border of the alveolus of M_3 – aboral border of the canine alveolus (+)

7)   Length of the cheektooth row, M_3-P_1, measured along the alveoli on the buccal side (+)

7a)   Length of the cheektooth row, M_3-P_2, measured along the alveoli on the buccal side (+)

8)   Length of the molar row, measured along the alveoli on the buccal side (–)

9)   Length of the premolar row, P_1-P_4, measured along the alveoli on the buccal side (–)

9a)   Length of the premolar row, P_2-P_4, measured along the alveoli on the buccal side (–)

10)   Length and breadth of M_3, measured near the base of the crown (Fig. 22a) (–)

11)   Length: oral border of the alveolus of P_2 – aboral border of the alveolus of I3 (+)

12)   Length of the median section of the body of mandible: from the mental prominence – Infradentale (+)

13)   Aboral height of the vertical ramus: Gonion ventrale – highest point of the condyle process (see Equus M 19) (+)

14)   Middle height of the vertical ramus: Gonion ventrale – deepest point of the mandibular notch. (see Equus M 20) (+)

15)   Oral height of the vertical ramus: Gonion ventrale – Coronion (see Equus M 21) (+)

16a)   Height of the mandible behind M_3, from the most aboral point of the alveolus (–)

16b)   Height of the mandible in front of M_1 (see note after Equus M 22c) (–)

16c)   Height of the mandible in front of P_2 (see note after Equus M 22c) (–)

(17)   Breadth of the two halves across the alveoli of the canine teeth. Not shown in Fig. 22b (+)

(18)   Breadth of the two halves between the most lateral points of the two angles = Gonion laterale – Gonion laterale. Not shown in Fig. 22b (+)

(19)   Breadth of the two halves between the condyle processes, measured between the most lateral points of the two condyle processes. Not shown in Fig. 22b (+)

(20)   Breadth of the two halves between the coronoid processes, measured between the most lateral points of the two coronoid processes. Not shown in Fig. 22b (–)

21)   Greatest diameter of the canine alveolus (+)

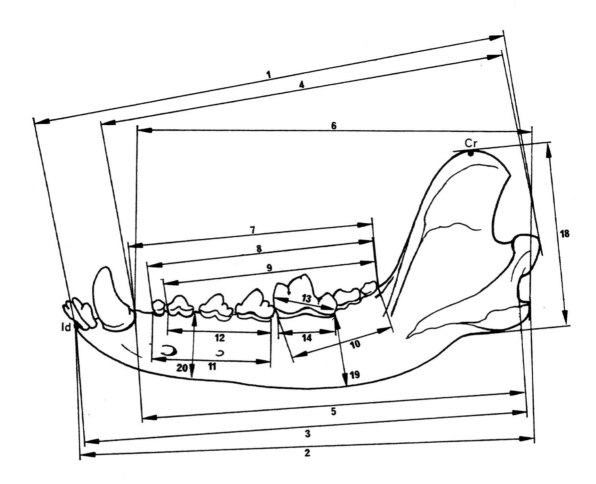

Figure 23a: <u>Canis</u> mandible, left side, lateral view.

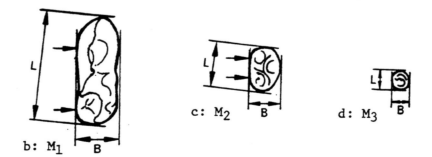

b: M_1 c: M_2 d: M_3

Figure 23b-d: <u>Canis</u> mandibular teeth,
length (L) and breadth (B), M 13, 15, 16.

Measurements of the mandible of <u>Canis</u> *(Fig. 23a,b,c,d)*

1) Total length: length from condyle process - Infradentale (+)
2) Length: the angular process - Infradentale (+)
3) Length from the indentation between the condyle process and the angular process - Infradentale (+)
4) Length: the condyle process - aboral border of the canine alveolus (+)
5) Length from the indentation between the condyle process and the angular process - aboral border of the canine alveolus (+)
6) Length: the angular process - aboral border of the canine alveolus (+)
7) Length: the aboral border of the alveolus of M_3 - aboral border of the canine alveolus (+)
8) Length of the cheektooth row, M_3-P_1, measured along the alveoli (+)
9) Length of the cheektooth row, M_3-P_2, measured along the alveoli (+)
10) Length of the molar row, measured along the alveoli (+)
11) Length of the premolar row, P_1-P_4, measured along the alveoli (-)
12) Length of the premolar row, P_2-P_4, measured along the alveoli (-)
13) Length and breadth of the carnassial, measured at the cingulum (Fig. 23b). If all teeth are in the alveoli, the length is best measured from dorsal (-)
14) Length of the carnassial alveolus (+)
15) Length and breadth of M_2, measured at the cingulum (Fig. 23c) (-)
16) Length and breadth of M_3, measured at the cingulum (Fig. 23d) (-)

Note: Single molars are easy to measure if they can be removed from the alveoli.

(17) Greatest thickness of the body of jaw (below M_1). Not shown in Fig. 23a (+)
18) Height of the vertical ramus: basal point of the angular process - Coronion (+)
19) Height of the mandible behind M_1, measured on the lingual side and at right angles to the basal border (-)
20) Height of the mandible between P_2 and P_3, measured on the lingual side and at right angles to the basal border (-)
(21) Height (length) of the canine, measured in a straight line from point to point. This measurement is only possible if the tooth can be removed from the jaw. Not shown in Fig. 23a (+)
(22) Calculation of the basal length (following Brinkmann 1924): measurement no. 2 multiplied by 1.21
(23) Calculation of the basal length (following Brinkmann 1924): measurement no. 4 multiplied by 1.37
(24) Calculation of the basal length (following Brinkmann 1924): measurement no. 5 multiplied by 1.46
(25) The mean of M 22, 23, and 24
(26) Calculation of the basal length (following Dahr 1937): measurement 8 multiplied by 2.9, minus 44 mm

Measurements of the mandible of <u>Ursus</u> (Figs. 16d,e,f,g and 23a) [see p. 46.]

1)-7) Same as <u>Canis</u> measurements

8) Length of the cheektooth row, P_4-M_3, measured along the alveoli (+)

9) Length of the molar row, measured along the alveoli (-)

10) Length and breadth of P_4, measured at the cingulum (Fig. 16d) (+)

11) Length and breadth of M_1, measured at the cingulum (Fig. 16e) (+)

12) Length and breadth of M_2, measured at the cingulum (Fig. 16f) (+)

13) Length and breadth of M_3, measured at the cingulum (Fig. 16g) (+)

14) Height of the vertical ramus: basal point of the angular process – Coronion (+)

15) Height of the mandible behind M_2, measured on the buccal side (-)

16) Height of the mandible between P_4 and M_1, measured on the buccal side (-)

(17) Height (length) of the canine, measured in a straight line from point to point. This measurement is only possible if the tooth can be removed from the jaw (+)

1) Total length: length from the condyle process – Infradentale (+)
2) Length from the indentation between the condyle process and the angular process – Infradentale (+)
3) Length: the condyle process – aboral border of the canine alveolus (+)
4) Length from the indentation between the condyle process and the angular process – aboral border of the canine alveolus (+)
5) Length of the cheektooth row, P_3–M_1, measured along the alveoli (+)
(6) Length and breadth of M_1, measured at the cingulum. Not shown in Fig. 24; measured in the same way as for dog (+)
7) Length of the carnassial alveolus (+)
8) Height of the vertical ramus: basal point of the angular process – Coronion (+)
9) Height of the mandible behind M_1, measured on the buccal side (+)
10) Height of the mandible in front of P_3, measured on the buccal side (+)

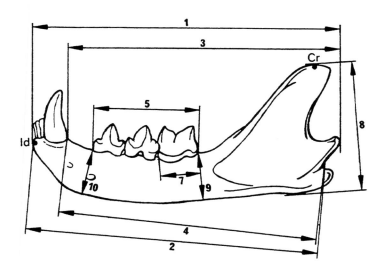

Figure 24: <u>Felis</u> mandible, left side, lateral view.

Measurements of the mandible of Lepus and Oryctolagus (Fig. 25)

1) Length from angle = greatest length: Gonion caudale - Infradentale (+)
2) Length of the cheektooth row, measured along the alveoli (+)
3) Length: aboral border of the alveolus of M_3 - Infradentale (+)
4) Length of the diastema: oral border of the alveolus of P_3 - Infradentale
5) Height of the vertical ramus: Gonion ventrale - highest point of the condyle process. Not to be measured in projection (see Hauser 1921, Fig. 10) (+)
5a) Height of the vertical ramus, measured in projection (see Duerst 1926, p. 333). Best done by placing one pointer of the slide gauge along the basal border of the mandible. This measurement can be taken precisely only if mandible is intact.

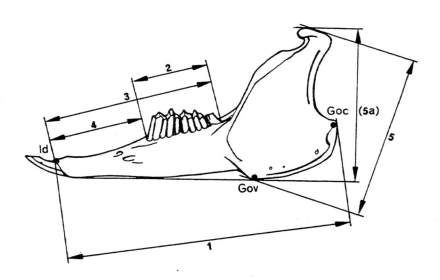

Figure 25: Lepus mandible, left side, lateral view.

POSTCRANIAL SKELETON

The *greatest length* of limb bones is measured in all cases from the most proximal prominent point to the most distal prominent point. But since in some bones these two points do not lie in the same axis (Fig. 26), one has to measure in such a way that the (imagined) longitudinal axis of the bone lies parallel to the scale of the measuring instrument. One thus measures the greatest length in projection. Such a procedure is easy with a bone whose shaft (corpus) is straight or almost straight (e.g., the radius of ruminants). More difficult to measure is the length of a bone whose shaft is curved or whose proximal and distal ends are twisted, facing in opposite directions (e.g., the radius of Sus).

The *breadth* measurements of proximal and distal ends of limb bones are measured from the most lateral prominent point to the most medial prominent point. In many bones this dimension is at right angles to the imagined longitudinal axis of the bone (Fig. 26a). There are, however, bones in which the most lateral and the most medial point lie in different planes, i.e., one of the two points lies more proximally or more distally than the other (e.g., the distal tibia of the bear, Fig. 26b). In such cases Duerst (1926, p. 463) suggests measurement in projection which is best accomplished by using a measuring box. But in our own experience this leads to very inexact results, especially when only the proximal or distal ends of the bones are present and one cannot establish the longitudinal axis of the bone. For that reason, we consider it surer to measure the direct distance from the most lateral to the most medial prominent point regardless of their positions. One measures therefore the diagonal rather than the breadth. The rare cases in which one should not measure the diagonal will be noted specifically (e.g., "greatest breadth" of astragalus of Equus).

Abbreviations instead of numbers are used for designating the measurements of bones of the mammalian postcranial skeleton and of the bird skeleton. The purpose of such abbreviations is to save time and space in the documentation of finds. Nouns are abbreviated with capital letters (e.g., L = length; C = corpus; F = facies) and adjectives with lower case letters (e.g., p = proximal; d = distal) except when they are at the beginning of an abbreviation (e.g., greatest length = GL). Unavoidably some few words which begin with the same letter will be abbreviated in the same way. Thus *diaphysis* is abbreviated with a "D" as is *depth,* but from the position of the letter in the abbreviation or from the abbreviation combination one can at once perceive which noun is meant. Generally one word is abbreviated to only one letter; in order to preserve clarity, however, this was not possible with all words (e.g., pe = *peripher* because p = *proximal,* just as cr = *cranial* and cd = *caudal).*

The abbreviations used to designate the measurements, moreover, have been designed to conform as much as possible to the usual German abbreviations. In order for this to be practicable, it was often necessary to refer to Latin terms. Complete uniformity could not be achieved with every word, however, and discrepancies occur in the following words:

English	German
D = depth	T = Tiefe
Di = diagonal	D = Durchmesser
C = circumference	U = Umfang
S = smallest	K = Kleinste

In addition, to permit this English compilation to serve as a guide to German osteoarchaeological publications, the German abbreviation immediately follows the English abbreviation where they differ.

NOTE: For the convenience of the user, illustrated parts of the post-cranial skeleton have been designated L (left) or R (right) in the upper right corner of each drawing where appropriate.

Figure 26a: <u>Ovis</u> radius.   Figure 26b: <u>Ursus</u> tibia.

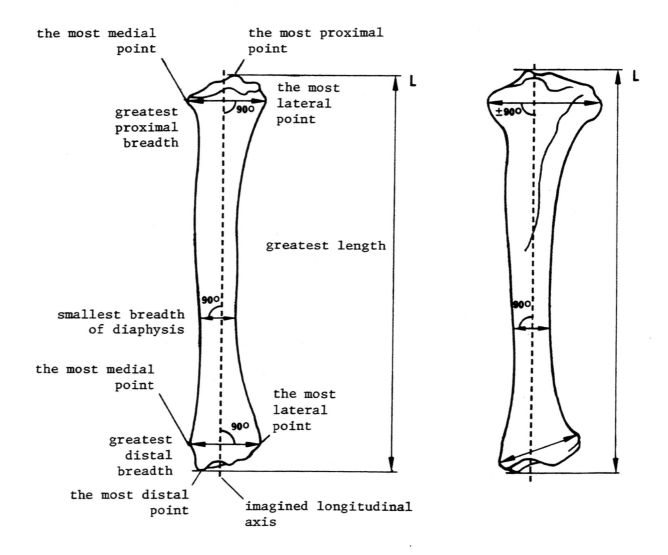

ATLAS (Fig. 27a-c)

GB   - Greatest breadth over the wings (+)

GL   - Greatest length (+)

BFcr   - (Greatest) breadth of the Facies articularis cranialis (= cranial
           articular surface) (+)

BFcd   - (Greatest) breadth of the Facies articularis caudalis (= caudal
           articular surface) (+)

GLF   - Greatest length from the Facies articularis cranialis to the
           Facies articularis caudalis (-)

LAd   - Length of the Arcus dorsalis (= dorsal arch), median. Measured
           only in carnivores (+)

H   - Height. Measured in a measuring box in such a way, that one
           lays the atlas with its cranial side on the bottom of the box
           and closes the blocks over the dorsal and ventral archs (+)

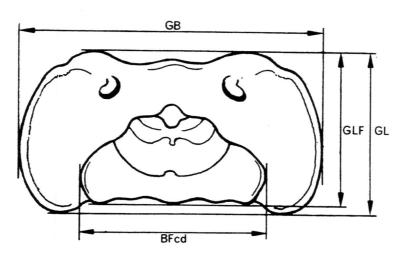

Figure 27a: <u>Bos</u> atlas, caudodorsal view.

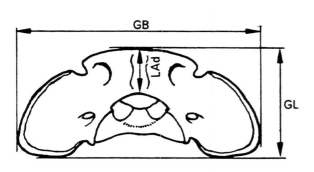

Figure 27b: <u>Canis</u> atlas, dorsal view.

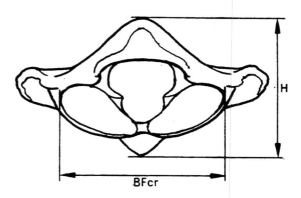

Figure 27c: <u>Sus</u> atlas, cranial view.

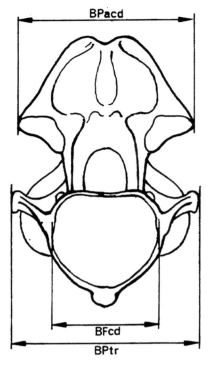

Figure 28a: Equus axis,
caudal view.

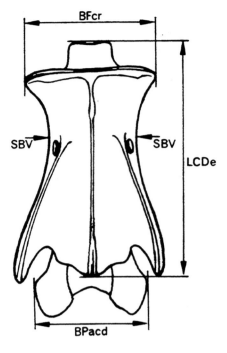

Figure 28b: Cervus axis,
ventral view.

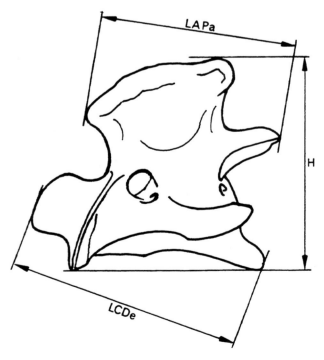

Figure 28c: Bos axis,
left side view.

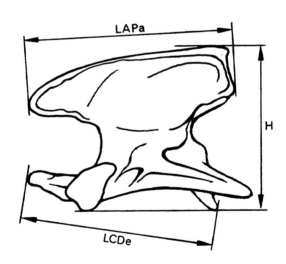

Figure 28d: Canis axis,
left side view.

AXIS (Fig. 28a-d)

LCDe   – (Greatest) length in the region of the corpus (= body) including the dens. If the caudal epiphysal plate has not yet fused, one measures without the caudal articular surface adding a note to that effect (+)

LAPa   – (Greatest) length of the arch including the Processus articulares caudales (+)

BFcr   – (Greatest) breadth of the Facies articularis cranialis (= cranial articular surface) (+)

BPacd   – (Greatest) breadth across the Processus articulares caudales (+)

BPtr   – (Greatest) breadth across the Processus transversi (+)

SBV   – KBW (German) = Smallest breadth of the vertebra (+)

BFcd   – (Greatest) breadth of the Facies terminalis caudalis (= caudal articular surface)

H   – (Greatest) height. Measured in a measuring box. One lays the two basal prominent points of the body of the vertebra on the fixed block of the instrument and closes the other block over the highest point of the spinous process (+)

SACRUM (Fig. 29a,b)

Since the number of segments in the sacrum can vary within a species, it is important to note the number of segments when recording measurements of length.

GL   – Greatest length on the ventral side: from the cranial borders of the wings to the caudoventral border of the body of the last vertebra (+)

PL   – Physiological length, measured between the centers of the bodies of the most cranial and the most caudal vertebrae (+)

GB   – Greatest breadth (across the wings) (+)

BFcr – (Greatest) breadth of the Facies terminalis cranialis (= cranial articular surface) (–)

HFcr – (Greatest) height of the Facies terminalis cranialis (–)

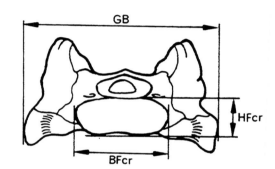

Figure 29a: <u>Canis</u> sacrum,
cranial view.

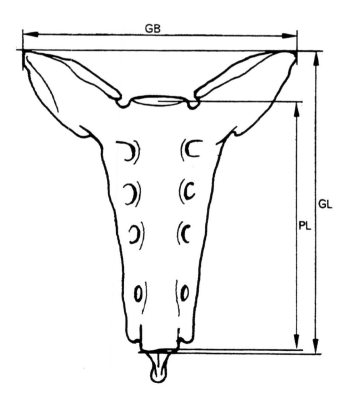

Figure 29b: <u>Equus</u> sacrum,
ventral view.

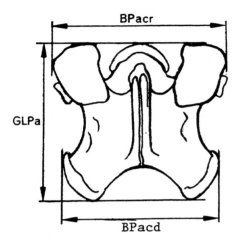

Figure 30a: <u>Ovis</u> cervical vertebra, dorsal view.

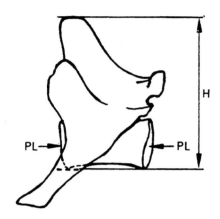

Figure 30b: <u>Canis</u> lumbar vertebra, left side view.

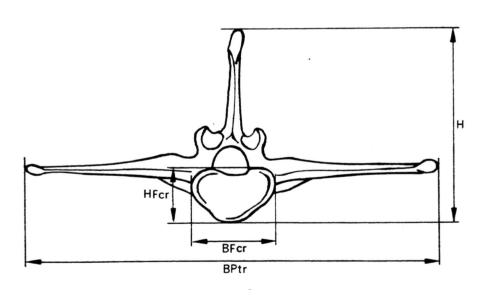

Figure 30c: <u>Equus</u> lumbar vertebra, cranial view.

PL   – Physiological length of the body. Measured between the centers of the Facies terminalis cranialis and the Facies terminalis caudalis (+)

GLPa   – Greatest length from the Processus articulares craniales to the Processus articulares caudales (in cervical vertebrae) (+)

BPacr   – (Greatest) breadth across the Processus articulares craniales (in cervical vertebrae) (+)

BPacd   – (Greatest) breadth across the Processus articulares caudales (in cervical vertebrae) (+)

BPtr   – (Greatest) breadth across the Processus transversi (+)

BF(cr/cd)   – (Greatest) breadth of the Facies terminalis cranialis/ caudalis (= cranial/caudal articular surface) (in thoracic vertebrae including the facets for the heads of the ribs) (–)

HF(cr/cd)   – (Greatest) height of the Facies terminalis cranialis/ caudalis (–)

H   – (Greatest) height

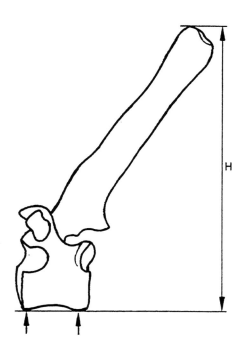

Figure 30d: <u>Equus</u> thoracic vertebra,
left side view.

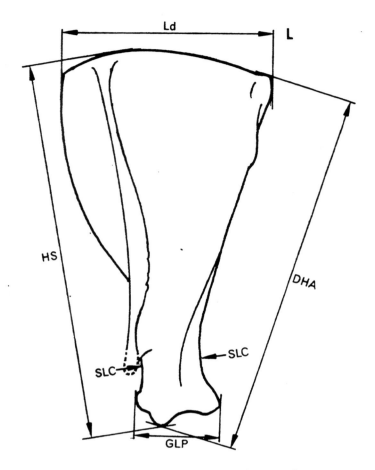

Figure 31a: <u>Bos</u> scapula, lateral view.

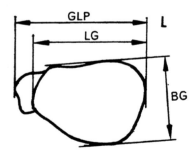

Figure 31b: <u>Bos</u> scapula,
distal view.

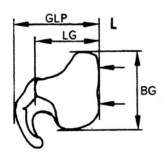

Figure 31c: <u>Lepus</u> scapula,
distal view.

SCAPULA (Fig. 31a-e)

HS — Height (see definitions of linear measurements p. 14) along the spine (+)

DHA — Diagonal height (see definitions of linear measurements p. 14): from the most distal point of the scapula to the thoracic angle (+). In scapulae where the thoracic angle is rounded (−)

Ld — (Greatest) dorsal length. Not to be measured in scapulae where one angle or both angles are rounded (+)

SLC — KLC (German) − Smallest length of the Collum scapulae (neck of the scapula). In general (+). Not easy to measure in scapulae of those ruminants which possess a crest on the aboral border of the neck (e.g., sheep). Not possible to measure in some species of carnivores.

GLP — Greatest length of the Processus articularis (glenoid process) (+)

LG — Length of the glenoid cavity. Measured to include the cranial lip of the glenoid cavity, parallel to the GLP, since one often cannot recognize the border of the glenoid cavity. Difficult to measure in pigs.

BG — Breadth of the glenoid cavity − Greatest breadth of the glenoid angle. (+)

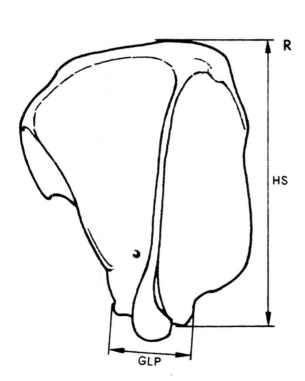
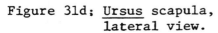

Figure 31d: <u>Ursus</u> scapula, lateral view.

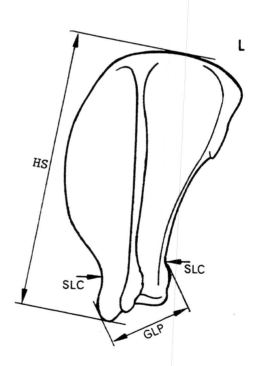

Figure 31e: <u>Canis</u> scapula, lateral view.

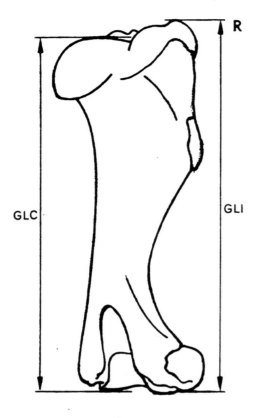

Figure 32a: <u>Equus</u> humerus,
caudolateral view.

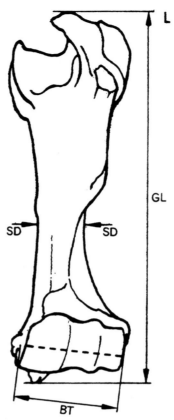

Figure 32b: <u>Bos</u> humerus,
cranial view.

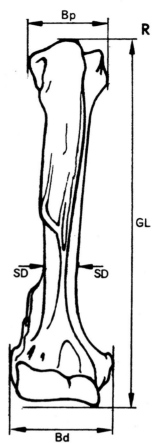

Figure 32c: <u>Ursus</u> humerus,
cranial view.

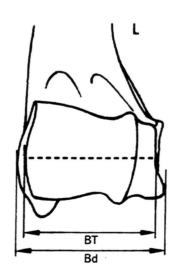

Figure 32d: <u>Cervus</u> humerus,
distal end,
cranial view.

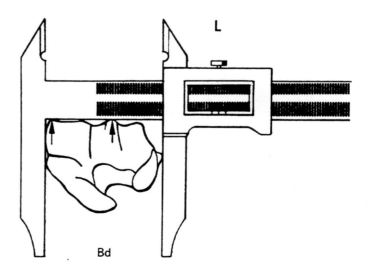

Figure 32e: <u>Bos</u> humerus,
distal view

HUMERUS (Fig. 32a-g)

GL - Greatest length (+)
GL1 - Greatest length of the lateral part (following Kiesewalter 1888):
      from the cranial part of the lateral tuberosity to the most distal
      point of the lateral border of the trochlea. Only in horses (+)
GLC - Greatest length from caput (head) (+)
Bp - (Greatest) breadth of the proximal end. Not in canids or lago-
      morphs (-)
Dp - Tp (German) - Depth of the proximal end. Only in canids and
      lagomorphs.
SD - KD (German) - Smallest breadth of diaphysis (+)
Bd - (Greatest) breadth of the distal end. Difficult to measure in
      ruminants and equids, because the most lateral and the most medial
      prominent points do not lie in the same plane and moreover the
      trochlea, especially in Bos, is oblique. If this distance is
      measured at right angles to the imagined longitudinal axis of
      the bone, the result is a disproportionately high value. This
      measurement is therefore to be taken in equids and ruminants as
      is shown in Figure 32e. A slide gauge with broad callipers must
      always be used (-)
BT - (Greatest) breadth of the trochlea. Only in equids and
      ruminants. The trochlea is measured in the middle from the
      cranial side including the outer borders of both the lateral and
      medial condyles (-)

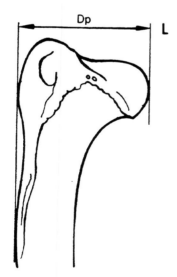

Figure 32f: <u>Canis</u> humerus,
            proximal end,
            lateral view.

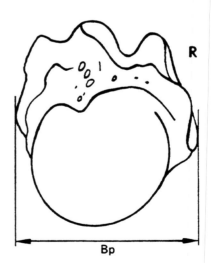

Figure 32g: <u>Equus</u> humerus,
            proximal view.

RADIUS AND ULNA (Fig. 33a-g)

Radius and Ulna:

GL - Greatest length
GL1 - Greatest length of lateral part (following Kiesewalter 1888, only
      in horses).

Radius:

GL - Greatest length (+)
PL - Physiological length. In general only in horses. One measures
      in the longitudinal axis of the bone from the proximal articular
      surface to the distal articular surface (+)
L1 - Length of the lateral part (following Kiesewalter 1888, only in
      horses) (+)
BP - (Greatest) breadth of the proximal end (+)
BFp - (Greatest) breadth of the Facies articularis proximalis (humeral
      articular surface). Measured in the same plane as Bp. Only in
      equids and ruminants (+)
SD - KD (German) - Smallest breadth of diaphysis. In radii in which
      the corpus is twisted (e.g., pig and bear), the alignment for the
      SD measurement is determined by the direction of the proximal
      articular surface (+)
CD - UD (German) - (Smallest) circumference of diaphysis. In general
      only in horses, where this measurement serves well to denote pro-
      portions (+)
Bd - (Greatest) breadth of the distal end (+)
BFd - (Greatest) breadth of the Facies articularis distalis. Measured
      in the same plane as Bd. Only in equids and ruminants (+)

Ulna:

GL - Greatest length (+)
LO - Length of the olecranon. Only in ruminants (-)
DPA - TPA (German) - Depth across the Processus anconaeus. One measures
      the shortest distance from the Processus anconaeus to the caudal
      border of the ulna (-)
SDO - KTO (German) - Smallest depth of the olecranon. Cannot be accurate-
      ly measured in bears.
BPC - (Greatest) breadth across the coronoid process ⩮ greatest breadth
      of the proximal articular surface (+)

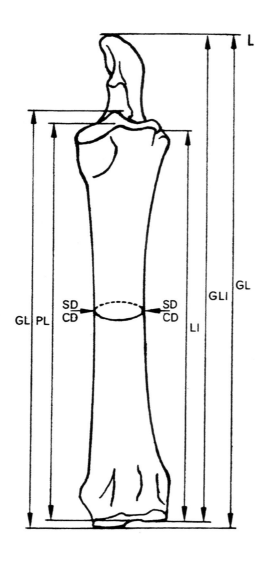

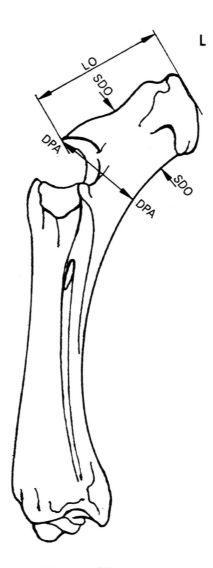

Figure 33a:
Equus radius and ulna,
dorsal view.

Figure 33b:
Bos radius and ulna,
lateral view.

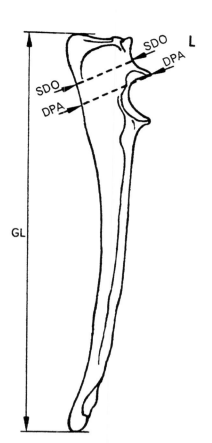

Figure 33c:
Canis ulna,
medial view.

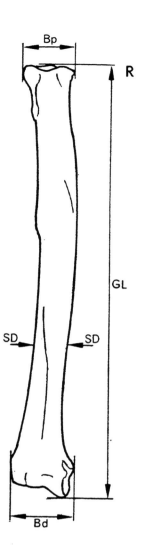
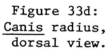

Figure 33d:
Canis radius,
dorsal view.

Figure 33e:
Cervus ulna,
proximal end,
dorsal view.

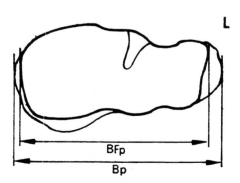

Figure 33f: Equus radius,
proximal view.

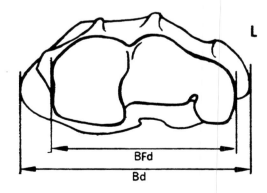

Figure 33g: Equus radius,
distal view.

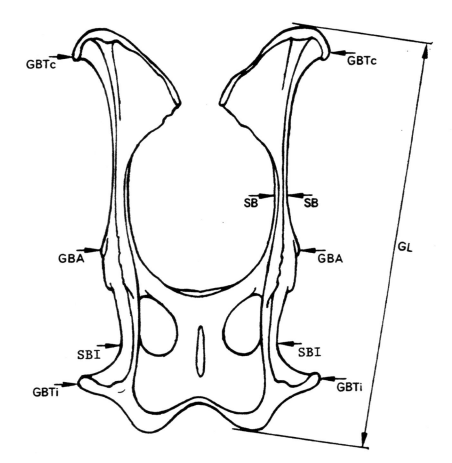

Figure 34a: *Ovis* pelvis, dorsal view.

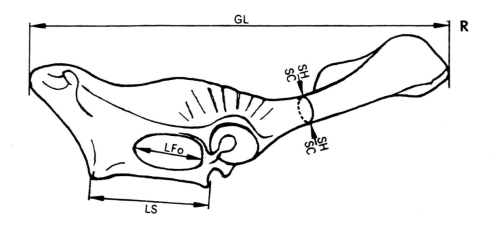

Figure 34b: *Sus* pelvis, lateral view.

PELVIS (Fig. 34a-d)

GL   – Greatest length of one half. Important: epiphyseal parts of the Tuber coxae and the Tuber ischiadicum must have fused! (+)

LA   – Length of the acetabulum including the lip (-). Measured only in species whose acetabulum forms a clear lip. In addition, one measures in horses and pigs, as well as in all other species which have no lip, the LAR

LAR – Length of the acetabulum on the rim (+)

LS   – Length of the symphysis. Only measured when the two halves have fused.

SH   – KH (German) – Smallest height of the shaft of ilium (+)

SB   – KB (German) – Smallest breadth of the shaft of ilium

SC   – KU (German) – Smallest circumference of the shaft of ilium

LFo – Inner length of the foramen obturatum (+)

GBTc – Greatest breadth across the Tubera coxarum – greatest breadth across the lateral angle (+)

GBA – Greatest breadth across the acetabula (+)

GBTi – Greatest breadth across the Tubera ischiadica (+)

SBI – KBI (German) – Smallest breadth across the bodies of the ischia (+)

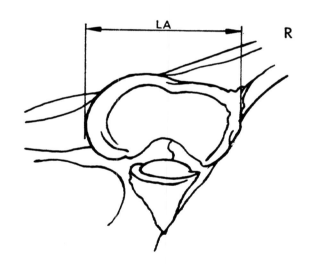 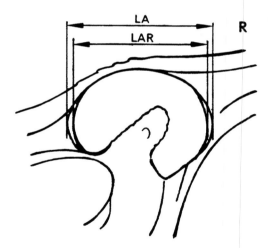

Figure 34c:
Bos pelvis,
acetabulum.

Figure 34d:
Equus pelvis,
acetabulum.

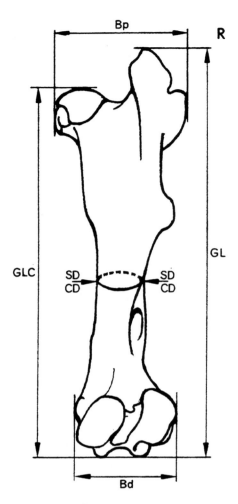

Figure 35a: Equus femur,
caudal view.

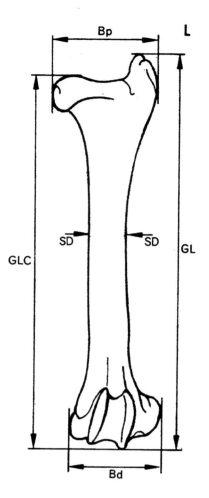

Figure 35b: Ovis femur,
cranial view.

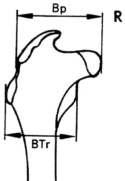

Figure 35c: Lepus femur,
proximal end,
cranial view.

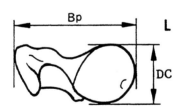

Figure 35d: Canis femur,
proximal view.

-84-

FEMUR (Fig. 35a-d)

GL   – Greatest length. In equids, ruminants, pigs, and lagomorphs
          = lateral length (+)

GLC – Greatest length from caput femoris (head). In some carnivore
          species = greatest length (+)

Bp   – (Greatest) breadth of the proximal end (+)

BTr – (Greatest) breadth of the region of the Trochanter tertius.
          Only in lagomorphs to be measured parallel to the Bp!

DC   – TC (German) – (Greatest) depth of the Caput femoris (+)

SD   – KD (German) – Smallest breadth of diaphysis (+)

CD   – UD (German) – (Smallest) circumference of diaphysis (see note
          to CD under "Radius and Ulna") (+)

Bd   – (Greatest) breadth of the distal end. In hoofed animals
          measured in a measuring box.

PATELLA (Fig. 36)

GL – Greatest length (+)
GB – Greatest breadth (+)

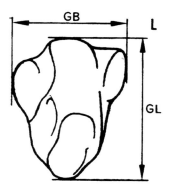

Figure 36: <u>Bos</u> patella,
cranial view.

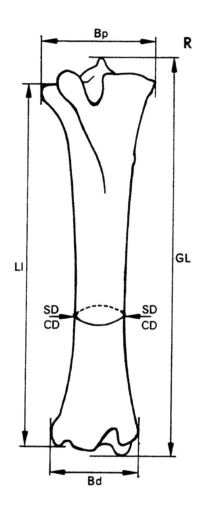

Figure 37a:
Equus tibia,
dorsal view.

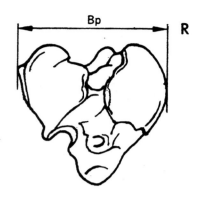

Figure 37b:
Capra tibia,
proximal view.

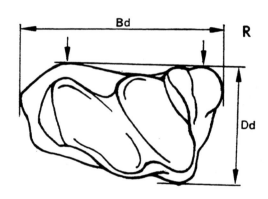

Figure 37c:
Equus tibia,
distal view.

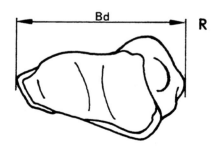

Figure 37d:
Ursus tibia,
distal view.

TIBIA (Fig. 37a-d)

GL – Greatest length (+)

Ll – Lateral length on the outer side (following Kiesewalter 1888, only in horses)

Bp – (Greatest) breadth of the proximal end (+)

SD – KD (German) – Smallest breadth of the diaphysis (+)

CD – UD (German) – (Smallest) circumference of the diaphysis (see note to CD under "Radius and Ulna") (+)

Bd – (Greatest) breadth of the distal end

Dd – Td (German) – (Greatest) depth of the distal end. Usually measured only in equids and lagomorphs.

FIBULA (Fig. 38)

GL – Greatest length (+)

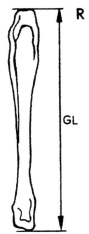

Figure 38: <u>Sus</u> Fibula, lateral view.

OS MALLEOLARE (Fig. 39)

GD – GT (German) – Greatest depth (+)

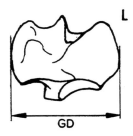

Figure 39: <u>Bos</u> Os malleolare, lateral view.

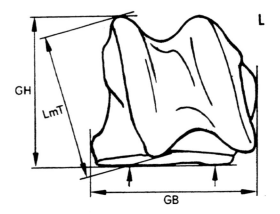

Figure 41a: <u>Equus</u> astragalus,
dorsal view.

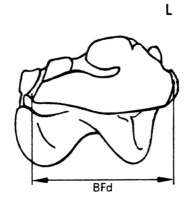

Figure 41b: <u>Equus</u> astragalus,
distal view.

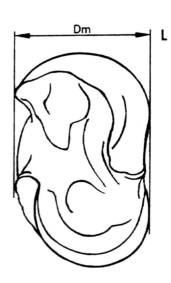

Figure 41c:
<u>Bos</u> astragalus,
medial view.

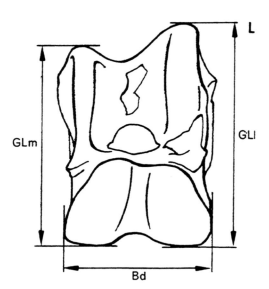

Figure 41d:
<u>Bos</u> astragalus,
dorsal view.

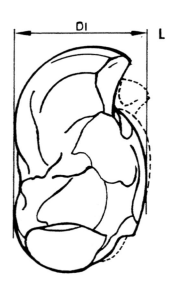

Figure 41e:
<u>Bos</u> astragalus,
lateral view.

Larger carpal bones (Fig. 40a-c)

GB – Greatest breadth. Measured in a measuring box or with a slide
gauge with broad callipers

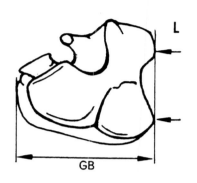

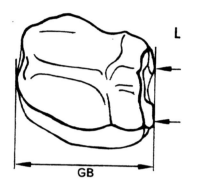

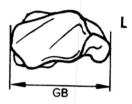

Figure 40a:
Equus
Os carpale 3

Figure 40b:
Bos
Os carpale 2+3

Figure 40c:
Canis
Os intermedio-
radiale

Astragalus (=talus) (equids) (Fig. 41a,b)

GH – Greatest height (= length). Measured in a measuring box (-)
GB – Greatest breadth. Only in a measuring box can an equid astrag-
     alus be accurately measured. One lays the distal side of the
     bone on the bottom of the box. The measurement is taken in
     projection (-)
BFd – Breadth of the Facies articularis distalis (distal articular
     surface) (+)
LmT – Length of the medial part of the Trochlea tali (+)

Astragalus (=talus) (Artiodactyla) (Fig. 41c-f)

GL1 – Greatest length of the lateral half (+)
GLm – Greatest length of the medial half (+)
Dl – Tl (German) – (Greatest) depth of the lateral half (+)
Dm – Tm (German) – (Greatest) depth of the medial half (-)
Bd – (Greatest) breadth of the distal end
Note: In Ovis, Capra, and Cervus there is a projection on the medial
     side in the middle between the proximal and the distal part of
     the astragalus. This makes it impossible to measure the Dm
     accurately. In the astragalus of the camel, also, the Dm and
     the Bd are impossible to measure precisely. Since the axis of
     the astragalus of Sus is slightly twisted, one takes only the
     two length measurements.

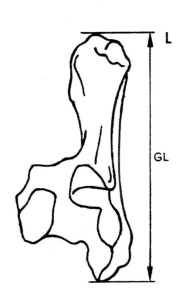

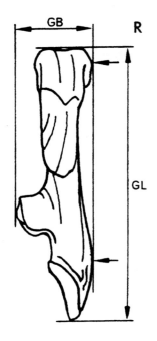

Figure 42a:
Equus calcaneus,
dorsal view.

Figure 42b:
Cervus calcaneus,
plantar view.

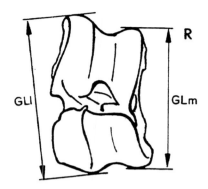

Figure 41f:
<u>Sus</u> astragalus,
dorsal view.

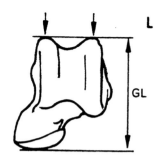

Figure 41g:
<u>Canis</u> astragalus,
dorsal view.

Astragalus (=talus) (carnivores and lagomorphs) (Fig. 41g)

GL - Greatest length (+)

Calcaneus (Fig. 42a,b)

GL - Greatest length (+)
GB - Greatest breadth. Measured in a measuring box or with a slide
     gauge with broad callipers

Other tarsal bones (Fig. 43a-c)

GB - Greatest breadth. Measured in a measuring box or with a slide
     gauge with broad callipers (+)

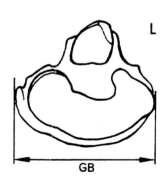

Figure 43a:
<u>Equus</u>
Os tarsale 3

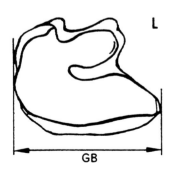

Figure 43b:
<u>Equus</u>
Os tarsi centrale

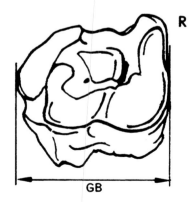

Figure 43c:
<u>Bos</u>
Os centrotarsale

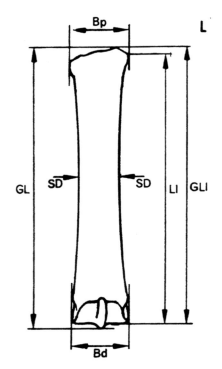

Figure 44a: <u>Equus</u>
Metacarpus III,
dorsal view.

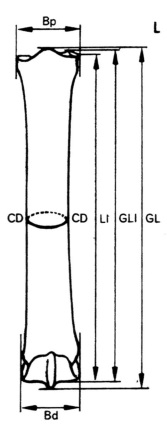

Figure 44b: <u>Equus</u>
Metatarsus III

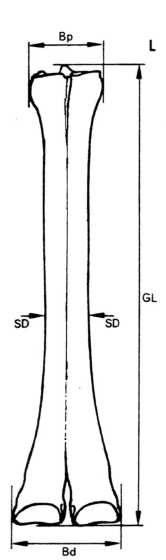

Figure 44c: <u>Camelus</u>
Metatarsus III+IV,
dorsal view.

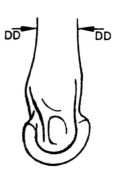

Figure 44d: <u>Capra</u>
Metatarsus III+IV,
side view.

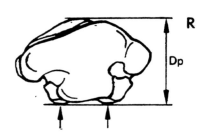

Figure 44e: <u>Equus</u>
Metacarpus III,
proximal view.

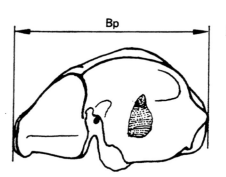

Figure 44f: <u>Bos</u>
Metacarpus III+IV,
proximal view.

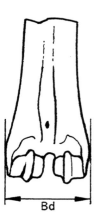

Figure 44g:
<u>Ovis</u>
Metatarsus
III+IV,
proximal view.

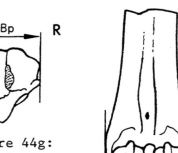

Figure 44h: <u>Bos</u>
Metatarsi III+IV,
dorsal view.

Equids and ruminants (Fig. 44a-i)

GL — Greatest length (+)

GL1 — Greatest length of the lateral part. Only in <u>Equus</u>. (+)

L1 — Lateral length on the outer side (following Kiesewalter 1888, only in horses)

Bp — (Greatest) breadth of the proximal end. The metatarsus in <u>Bos</u> is measured in such a way that the plantar border of the proximal articular surface lies parallel to the scale of the measuring instrument (Fig. 44i, below) (+)

Dp — Tp (German) — (Greatest) depth of the proximal end. Usually only in equids where it is easy to measure only in the metacarpus.

SD — KD (German) — Smallest breadth of the diaphysis (+)

CD — UD (German) — (Smallest) circumference of the diaphysis (see note to CD under "Radius and Ulna") (+)

DD — TD (German) — (Smallest) depth of the diaphysis

Bd — (Greatest) breadth of the distal end (+)

Dd — Td (German) — (Greatest) depth of the distal end. Usually only in equids (+)

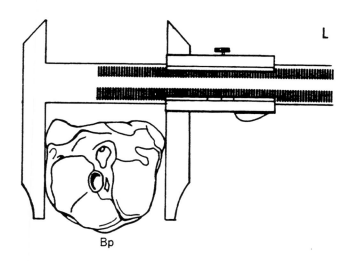

Figure 44i: <u>Bos</u> metatarsus III+IV,
proximal view.

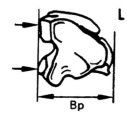

Figure 44j:
Sus
Metacarpus III,
proximal view.

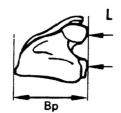

Figure 44k:
Sus
Metacarpus IV,
proximal view.

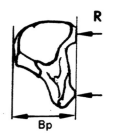

Figure 44l:
Sus
Metatarsus III,
proximal view.

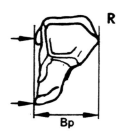

Figure 44m:
Sus
Metatarsus IV,
proximal view.

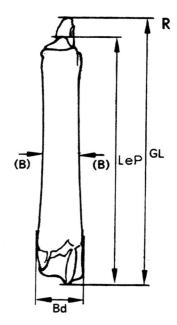

Figure 44n:
Sus
Metatarsus IV,
dorsal view.

Sus (Fig. 44j-n)

Note: For the second and fifth metapodial bones one measures only
      the GL

GL - Greatest length (-)
LeP - LoP (German) - Length excepting thè plantar projection (+)
Bp - (Greatest) breadth of the proximal end. The fixed points
      for one of the callipers are the two small articular facets
      on the inner or axial border of the proximal end (-)
B   - Breadth in the middle of the diaphysis (-)
Note: Bp and B are unusual measurements. Many research workers do
      not take them.
Bd - (Greatest) breadth of the distal end (+)

Carnivores and lagomorphs (Fig. 44o)

GL - Greatest length (+)
Bd - (Greatest) breadth of the distal end (+)

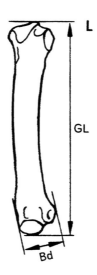

Figure 44o:
Canis Metacarpus V,
dorsal view.

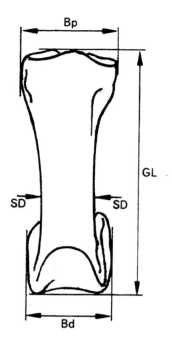

Figure 45c: <u>Camelus</u>
Phalanx 1, dorsal view.

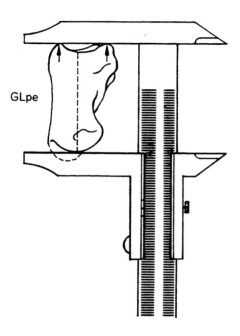

Figure 45d: <u>Bos</u> phalanx 1,
anterior, peripheral view.

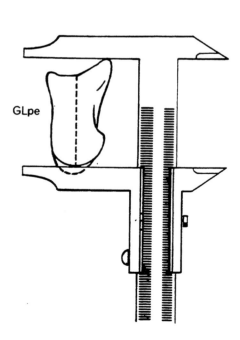

Figure 45e: <u>Bos</u> phalanx 1,
posterior, peripheral view.

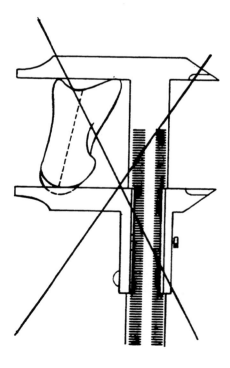

Figure 45f: <u>Bos</u> phalanx 1,
posterior, peripheral view.

PHALANX I (Fig. 45a-f)

Equids (Fig. 45a,b)

GL – Greatest length (measuring box!) (+)
Bp – (Greatest) breadth of the proximal end (+)
BFp – (Greatest) breadth of the Facies articularis proximalis
       (proximal articular surface) (+)
Dp – Tp (German) – Depth of the proximal end (+)
SD – KD (German) – Smallest breadth of the diaphysis (+)
Bd – (Greatest) breadth of the distal end (+)
BFd – (Greatest) breadth of the Facies articularis distalis (+)

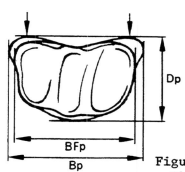

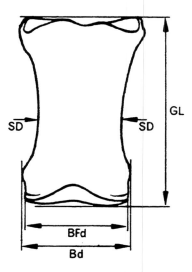

Figure 45b: <u>Equus</u>
    Phalanx 1,
    dorsal view.

Figure 45a: <u>Equus</u>
    Phalanx 1, proximal view.

Camel (Fig. 45c), carnivores, and lagomorphs

GL – Greatest length (+)
Bp – (Greatest) breadth of the proximal end (+)
SD – KD (German) – Smallest breadth of the diaphysis (+)
Bd – (Greatest) breadth of the distal end (+)

Bovids and <u>Sus</u> (Fig. 45d-f)

GLpe – Greatest length of the peripheral (abaxial) half. Most of the
       anterior first phalanges of <u>Bos</u> are formed in such a manner
       that the proximodorsal and the proximovolar prominent parts
       of the peripheral section of the proximal articular surface
       can serve as fixed points for one of the callipers. If one
       were to measure the posterior phalanges in the same way, many
       of them would be oriented obliquely in the measuring instrument.
       One has to hold these bones in such a way that the (imagined)
       longitudinal axis of the bone lies parallel to the measuring
       scale (Fig. 45e, not Fig. 45f) (−)
Bp   – (Greatest) breadth of the proximal end (+)
SD   – KD (German) – Smallest breadth of the diaphysis (−)
Bd   – (Greatest) breadth of the distal end (+)

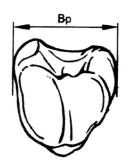

Figure 46c: <u>Bos</u>
Phalanx 2,
proximal view.

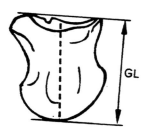

Figure 46d: <u>Bos</u>
Phalanx 2,
peripheral view.

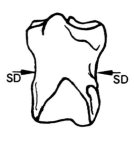

Figure 46e: <u>Bos</u>
Phalanx 2,
dorsal view.

Figure 46f: <u>Bos</u>
Phalanx 2,
volar/plantar view.

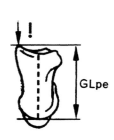

Figure 46g: <u>Capra</u>
Phalanx 2,
peripheral view.

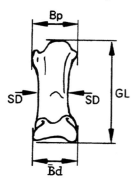

Figure 46h: <u>Canis</u>
Phalanx 2,
dorsal view.

PHALANX 2 (Fig. 46a-h)

Equids (Fig. 46a,b)

GL – Greatest length (measuring box!) (+)
Bp – (Greatest) breadth of the proximal end (+)
BFp – (Greatest) breadth of the Facies articularis proximalis
      (proximal articular surface) (+)
Dp – Tp (German) – Depth of the proximal end (+)
SD – KD (German) – Smallest breadth of the diaphysis (+)
Bd – (Greatest) breadth of the distal end (+)

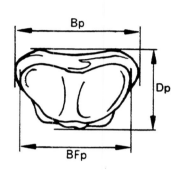

Figure 46a: <u>Equus</u>
Phalanx 2,
proximal view.

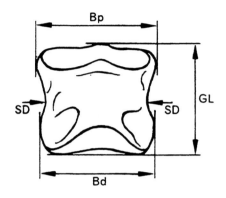

Figure 46b: <u>Equus</u>
Phalanx 2,
dorsal view.

Other species (Fig. 46c-h)

GL – Greatest length. In ruminants = greatest length of the peri-
      pheral (abaxial) half. As in Phalanx 1, the (imagined) longi-
      tudinal axis of the bone has to lie parallel to the scale of
      the measuring instrument
Bp – (Greatest) breadth of the proximal end (+)
SD – KD (German) – Smallest breadth of the diaphysis (–)
Bd – (Greatest) breadth of the distal end (+)

NAVICULAR (DISTAL SESAMOID BONE) OF EQUIDS (Fig. 47)

GB – Greatest breadth (+)

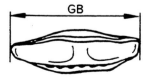

Figure 47: <u>Equus</u> distal sesamoid

PHALANX 3 (Fig. 48a-d)

Equids (Fig. 48a,b)

GL – Greatest length (+)
GB – Greatest breadth (+)
LF – Length of the Facies articularis (articular surface) (–)
BF – Breadth of the Facies articularis (–)
Ld – Length of the dorsal surface (+)
HP – Height in the region of the extensor process (measuring box!) (+)

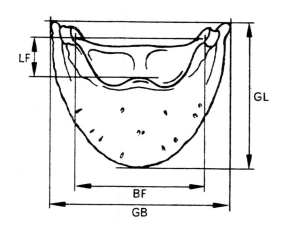

Figure 48a: <u>Equus</u>
Phalanx 3,
dorsoproximal view.

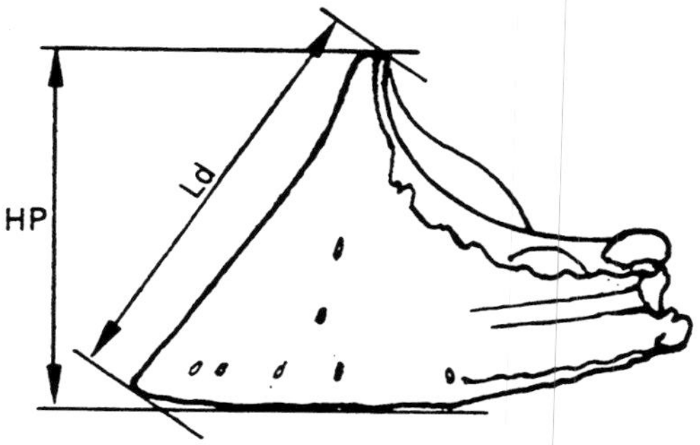

Figure 48b: <u>Equus</u>
Phalanx 3,
side view.

Ruminants and <u>Sus</u> (Fig. 48c,d)

DLS – (Greatest) diagonal length of the sole (+)
Ld – Length of the dorsal surface (+)
MBS – Middle breadth of the sole = breadth in the middle of the
      sole (+)

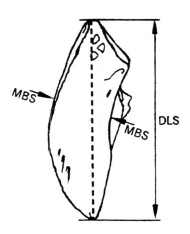

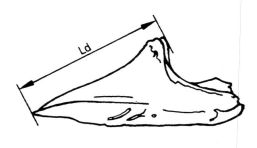

Figure 48c: <u>Bos</u>
Phalanx 3,
view of sole.

Figure 48d: <u>Bos</u>
Phalanx 3,
peripheral view.

PART THREE

MEASUREMENT OF THE BIRD SKELETON

GENERAL

The measurement of bird bones from site refuse is only beginning to be
carried out. It is just as necessary for distinguishing the species and
for the documentation of size and variation as is the measurement of
mammal bones and should be dealt with in the same way.

The primary sources for the following guide to the measurement of bird
bones are five comparative morphological investigations carried out on
the bones of recent birds: Bacher 1967, Woelfle 1967, Erbersdobler 1968,
Kraft 1972, and Fick 1974. These studies have been undertaken in the
Institute of Palaeoanatomy at the University of Munich under the guidance
of J. Boessneck. In the first three papers only measurements for bones
of the postcranial skeleton are defined and explained with diagrams. The
last two papers deal also with the skull. It is obvious that for special
investigations more measurements may become necessary (e.g., Ballmann
1966, pp. 35 ff.)

Reference to these five studies will show that they do not utilize a
standard nomenclature. The reason for this is the nonuniformity of the
nomenclature in the previously published literature. Nevertheless each
of the five authors tried to be consistent in his own work, explaining all
terminology additionally by diagrams, so that each of the works, considered separately, is clear and comprehensible. Misunderstandings may arise
only when one work is compared with another. This state of affairs
demonstrates how very necessary it is to standardize nomenclature in the
osteology of birds.

Apart from the general nonuniformity in the nomenclature, special
complications arise in the designation of measurements for bird bones.
The bones of the wings, whether adjacent to the body or extended, have
different positions in relation to the body than do the bones of the
forelimbs of mammals (Fig. 3). This situation leads, if one refers to

the (whole) skeleton, to different definitions for the directions (see Kraft 1972). For the sake of standardization, however, one should use for birds the same scheme as for mammals. One should not follow the change in the definitions of *breadth* and *depth* proposed by Kraft (1972).

The following measurements represent only a selection. The selection was chosen primarily with an eye to being able to compare measurements with those from bird bones found in the literature. Only data for prehistoric and early historic bird bones from alluvial times have been taken into consideration (e.g., Schweizer 1961, Dräger 1964, Schülke 1965, Müller 1967, Sauer-Neubert 1969, Hornberger 1970, Kühnhold 1971, Küpper 1972). Furthermore, an effort was made to choose measurements which can be taken in the same way for the bones of all bird species living in Europe. Since the bones of the different bird species, and especially the skulls, differ considerably in shape, the selection of dimensions which can be measured in the same way is limited. Each research worker must decide for himself whether he wants to add other dimensions which he then must define exactly and, if need be, explain by diagrams.

The following compilation is based primarily on experience gained while dealing with the bones of the domestic hen (the most frequently encountered avian remains of pre- and early historic sites) as well as from the bones of geese and ducks. The instructions are therefore applicable mainly to the bones of these birds. Much rarer than the bones of hens, geese, and ducks are the bones of pigeons and crows. Only in exceptional cases do the bones of any other bird families occur more frequently than these five in site refuse.

SKULL

CRANIUM (Fig. 49a-e)

GL – Greatest length: Protuberantia occipitalis externa – Apex
      praemaxillaris (+)
CBL – Condylobasal length: aboral border of the occipital condyle –
      Apex praemaxillaris (+)
GB – Greatest breadth, wherever it is to be found, usually across
      the Processus postfrontales (+)
GBP – Greatest breadth across the Processus postfrontales (+)
SBO – KBO (German) – Smallest breadth between the orbits on the
      dorsal side = smallest breadth of the Pars nasalis of the
      Frontale (+)
GH – Greatest height in the median plane: from the Basitemporale
      in the median plane to the highest and median point of the
      braincase. One calliper lies on the nasal or ventral point
      of the Basitemporale (–)

     In most species, the following measurements can also be taken:

LP – Length from the Protuberantia occipitalis externa to the most
      aboral points of the Processus frontales of the Incisivum in
      the median plane
LI – (Greatest) length of the Incisivum: Apex praemaxillaris – most
      aboral points of the Processus frontales of the Incisivum in
      the median plane

Parts of and points on the cranium (Fig. 49):

1 = Protuberantia occipitalis externa
2 = Apex praemaxillaris
3 = Processus postfrontalis
4 = Pars nasalis of the frontal bone
5 = Processus frontalis of the praemaxilla
6 = Basitemporale (= Basisphenoid)
7 = Linea nuchalis superior
8 = Condylus occipitalis

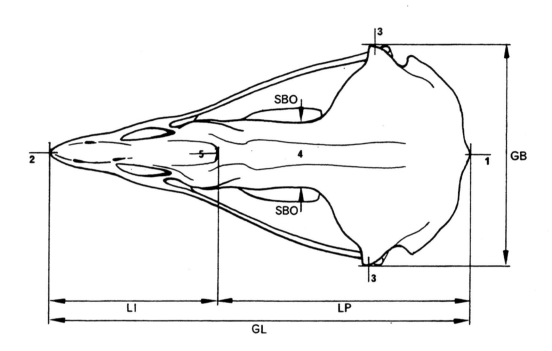

Figure 49a: Cranium of <u>Aquila</u>, dorsal view.

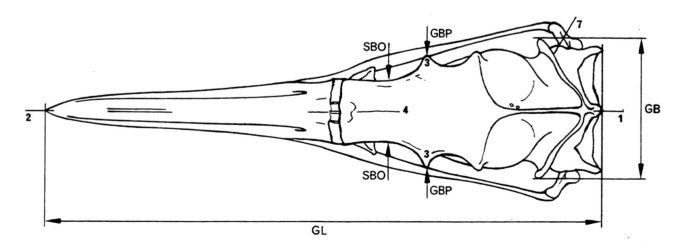

Figure 49b: Cranium of <u>Phalacrocorax</u>, dorsal view.

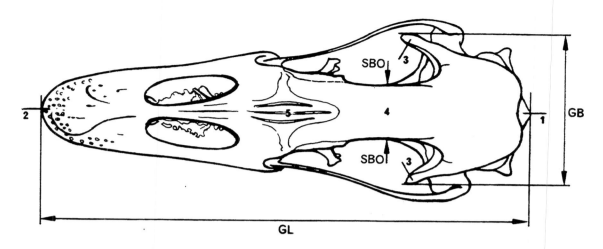

Figure 49c: Cranium of _Anser_, dorsal view.

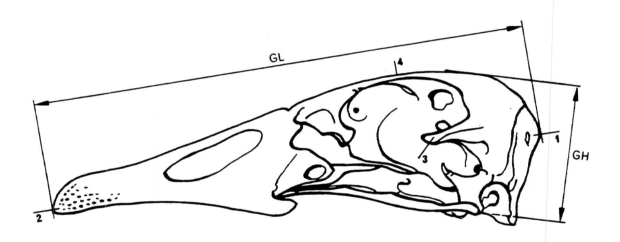

Figure 49d: Cranium of _Anser_, left side view.

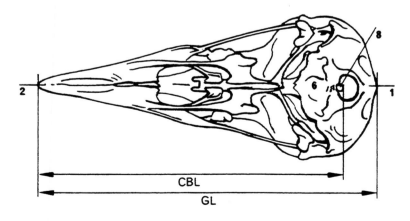

Figure 49e: Cranium of _Gallus_, basal view.

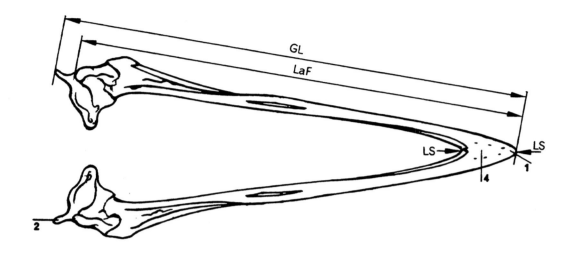

Figure 50a: Mandible of <u>Otis</u>, dorsal view.

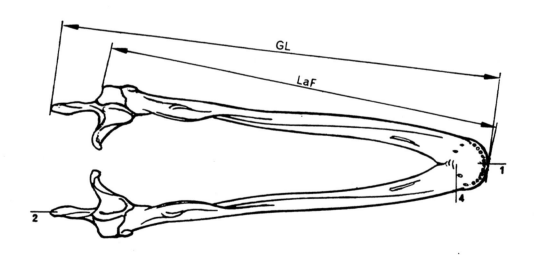

Figure 50b: Mandible of <u>Anser</u>, dorsal view.

MANDIBLE (Fig. 50a-c)

GL   – Greatest length of one-half of the mandible: Apex to the most
        aboral point of the mandible (+)

LaF – Length from the most aboral point of the Facies articularis
        (= articular surface) on one side to the Apex

        In those species in which the inner border of the Symphysis
        forms a wide open angle, one can measure the

LS   – Length of the Symphysis

Parts of and points on the mandible (Fig. 50):

    1 = Apex
    2 = Processus aboralis
    3 = Processus lateralis
    4 = Symphysis mandibulae

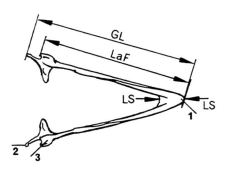

Figure 50c: Mandible of <u>Alectoris</u>,
dorsal view.

Parts of and points on the sternum (Fig. 51):

1 = Manubrium sterni
2 = Labium ventrale s. externum
3 = Labium dorsale s. internum
4 = Crista sterni s. Carina
5 = Apex cristae sterni
6 = Metasternum
7 = Facets of the costosternal articles

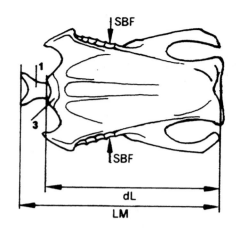

Figure 51a: Sternum of
Corvus, dorsal view.

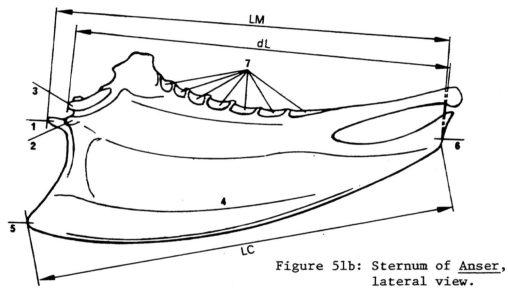

Figure 51b: Sternum of Anser,
lateral view.

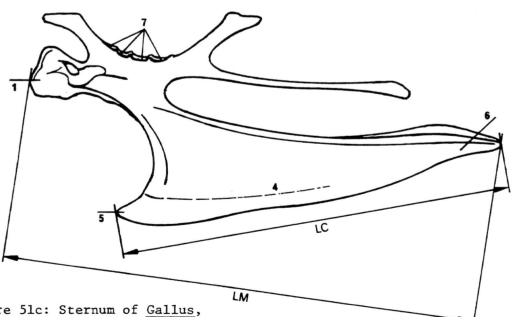

Figure 51c: Sternum of Gallus,
lateral view.

STERNUM (Fig. 51a-d)

LM — Length from the Manubrium sterni: from the cranial point of the
     Manubrium sterni (or the median point of the line joining the
     cranial points of the Manubrium sterni) to the caudal border (or
     point) of the Metasternum in the median plane (+)

dL — Dorsal length: from the cranial point of the Labium dorsale
     or internum (or the median point of the line joining the cranial
     points of the labia) to the caudal border (or point) of the
     Metasternum in the median plane

Note: In some species (e.g., Galliformes and Anseriformes) the LM
     is almost the same as the dL

LC — Length of the Crista sterni: from the Apex cristae sterni
     to the caudal border (or point) of the Metasternum in the
     median plane (+). In some species the Crista sterni disappears
     before reaching the caudal border of the Metasternum. Never-
     theless one has to measure to the Metasternum, because no fixed
     points exist at the caudal end of the Crista sterni.

SBF — KBF (German) — Smallest breadth between the facets for the costo-
     sternal articulations, measured at the narrowest part (+)

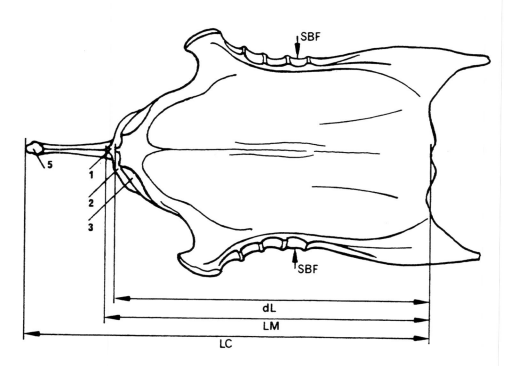

Figure 51d: Sternum of <u>Phalacrocorax</u>,
            dorsal view.

l = Processus lateralis

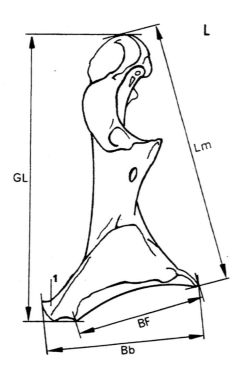

Figure 52a: Coracoid of Aquila,
caudal view.

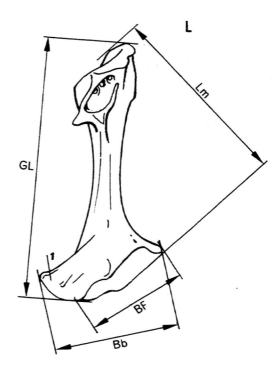

Figure 52b: Coracoid of Sula,
caudal view.

CORACOID (Fig. 52a-d)

GL – Greatest (diagonal) length (+). Measured generally to the distal
    point of the basal articular surface, exceptionally to the distal
    point of the Processus lateralis (e.g., in eagles and ganets).
Lm – medial length (+)
Bb – (Greatest) basal breadth (+)*
BF – Breadth of the Facies articularis basalis (= basal articular
    surface) (+)**
Note: In the Apodidae, Bb = BF.

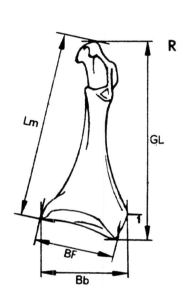

Figure 52c:
Coracoid of <u>Anas</u>,
caudal view.

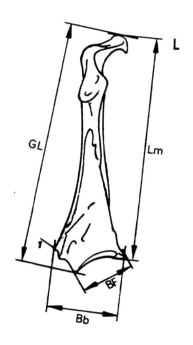

Figure 52d:
Coracoid of <u>Gallus</u>,
caudal view.

*Bacher (1967, p. 11) and Erbersdobler (1968, p. 10) designate this
measurement as DD – Durchmesser distal (=distal diameter).

**This measurement is designated by the same two authors as BB – basale
  Breite (=basal breadth). These designations have been adopted by some
  other authors, a fact which must be taken into account when making
  comparisons with the literature.

SCAPULA (Fig. 53a-c)

GL – Greatest length (+)
Dic – Dc (German) – (Greatest) cranial diagonal (–)*

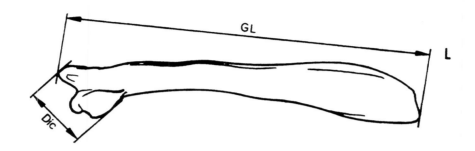

Figure 53a: Scapula of <u>Otis</u>,
dorsolateral view.

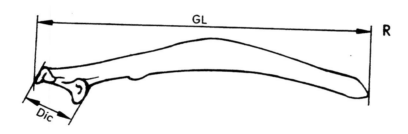

Figure 53b: Scapula of <u>Gallus</u>,
ventromedial view.

Figure 53c: Scapula of <u>Corvus</u>,
cranial view.

*Erbersdobler (1968, p. 11) designates this measurement as BC – Breite
cranial (=cranial breadth).

Parts of and points on the humerus (Fig. 54):

1 = Tuberculum mediale s. ventrale
2 = Tuberculum laterale s. dorsale
3 = Processus supracondylicus radialis
4 = Crista lateralis

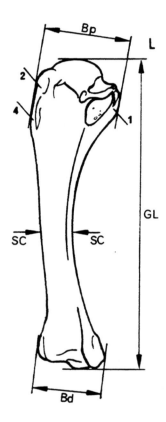

Figure 54a:
Humerus of
Gallus,
medial or
ventral view.

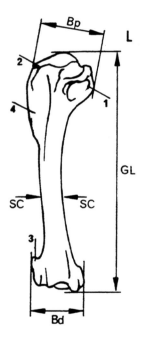

Figure 54b:
Humerus of
Corvus,
medial or
ventral view.

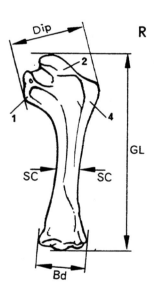

Figure 54c:
Humerus of
Columba,
medial or
ventral view.

HUMERUS (Fig. 54a-d)

GL - Greatest length (+)

Bp - Breadth of the proximal end from the Tuberculum laterale or dorsale to the Tuberculum mediale or ventrale, without the Crista lateralis. One measures the greatest distance although this measurement is not at right angles to the longitudinal axis of the bone (-)

Note: At the proximal end of the humerus of the pigeon Fick (1974, p. 21) measures only the Dip - proximal diagonal. Also in small birds one can measure only the Dip - i.e., the proximal breadth including the Crista lateralis.

SC - KC (German) - Smallest breadth of the corpus (+)*

Bd - (Greatest) breadth of the distal end. Measured without the Processus supracondylicus radialis, which one can find in some species (Procellariiformes, Charadriiformes, Passeriformes) at the distal end of the corpus. This measurement is best taken from the distal aspect (+)

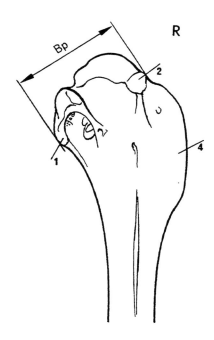

Figure 54d: Humerus of Otis,
proximal end, medial
or ventral view.

*Many authors designate this measurement as KS - Kleinste Breite des Schaftes (=Smallest breadth of the shaft).

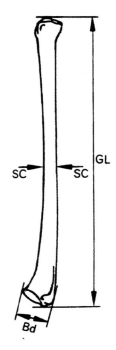

Figure 55: Radius
of Gallus.

Parts of and points on the ulna (Fig. 56):

1 = Olecranon
2 = Facies articularis medialis s. ventralis
3 = Facies articularis lateralis s. dorsalis

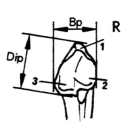

Figure 56a:
Ulna of
Gallus,
proximal end.

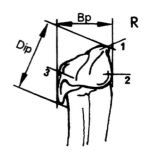

Figure 56b:
Ulna of
Phalacrocorax,
proximal end.

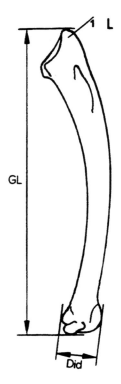

Figure 56c:
Ulna of
Gallus.

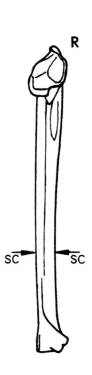

Figure 56d:
Ulna of
Gallus.

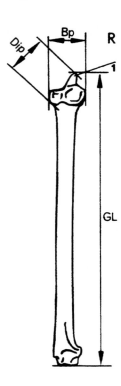

Figure 56e:
Ulna of
Corvus.

RADIUS (Fig. 55)

GL - Greatest length (+)
SC - KC (German) - Smallest breadth of the corpus (-)*
Bd - (Greatest) breadth of the distal end (+)

ULNA (Fig. 56a-e)

GL - Greatest length (+)
Dip - Dp (German) - (Greatest) diagonal of the proximal end from the
      caudal border of the Olecranon to the cranial border of the Facies
      articularis lateralis or dorsalis (-)**
Bp - (Greatest) breadth of the proximal end from the Facies articularis
      medialis or ventralis to the Facies articularis lateralis or
      dorsalis (-)**
SC - KC (German) - Smallest breadth of the corpus. This measurement
      is easy to take in ulnae of Galliformes because the corpus is
      compressed from both sides. One measures the narrowest part of
      the compression. This measurement cannot be taken exactly in
      birds where the corpus of the ulna is round. It therefore has
      to be either omitted or redefined as the case may be.***
Did - Dd (German) - (Greatest) diagonal of the distal end (+)

*   See note to SC of the Humerus
** Important: Bacher (1967, Fig. 5) measures the Bp in the same way as
    is explained here, but measures the Dip in a completely different way.
    Erbersdobler (1968, Fig. 6) measures the Dip in the same way as is
    shown here, but measures the Bp in a completely different way. This
    must be taken into consideration when comparing literature for which
    the data of these two authors form the basis.
***See note to SC of the Humerus

Parts of and points on the carpometacarpus (Fig. 57):

1 = Os metacarpale I
2 = Os metacarpale II
3 = Os metacarpale III
4 = Processus distalis

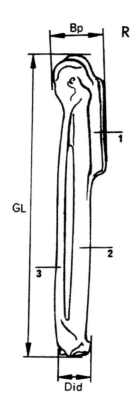

Figure 57a:
Carpometacarpus
of Gavia.

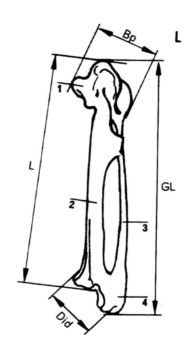

Figure 57b:
Carpometacarpus
of Corvus.

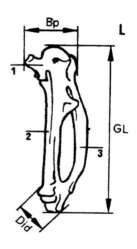

Figure 57c:
Carpometacarpus
of Gallus.

CARPOMETACARPUS (Fig. 57a-c)

GL — Greatest length (+)
L   — Length of the metacarpus II, from articular surface to articular
      surface without the Processus distalis. Only measured in birds
      where a distinctly developed Processus distalis is to be found,
      e.g., in Passeriformes
Bp — (Greatest) breadth of the proximal extremity. One measures the
      greatest distance although this measurement is in some species
      more diagonal than at right angles to the longitudinal axis of
      the bone (+)
Did — Dd (German) — Diagonal of the distal end. One measures only the
      distal articular surface. This measurement lies at right angles
      to the longitudinal axis of the bone in birds which do not possess
      a Processus distalis. In birds which possess a Processus distalis
      this measurement is not taken at right angles to the longitudinal
      axis.

PHALANX 1 ANTERIOR OF THE 2ND DIGIT (Fig. 58)

GL — Greatest length (−)
L — Length from articular surface to articular surface (+)

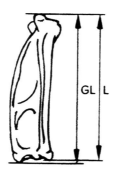

Figure 58:
Phalanx 1 anterior
of Anser,
digit II.

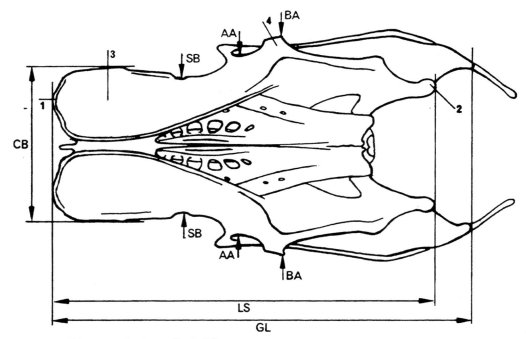

Figure 59a: Pelvis of Gallus,
            dorsal view.

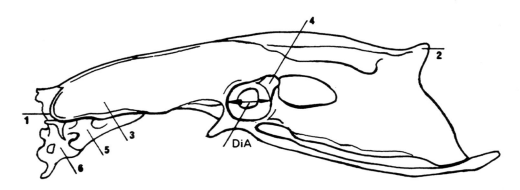

Figure 59b: Pelvis of Gallus,
            lateral view.

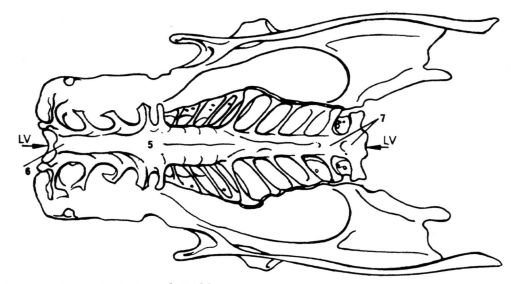

Figure 59c: Pelvis of Gallus,
            ventral view.

PELVIS (Fig. 59a-f)

GL   - Greatest length (without pubis): cranial border of the ilia
          (= Margo iliocranialis) - most caudal points of the ischia

LS   - Length from the cranial border of the ilia to the Spinae ilio-
          caudales. Measured only in species which have distinctly
          developed Spinae iliocaudales.

Note: In some species, the LS = GL

LV   - Length along the vertebrae, centrally = length of the Os
          lumbosacrale, from the most cranial (thoracic) vertebra fused
          with the Os lumbosacrale to the most caudal (coccygeal) verte-
          bra fused with the Os lumbosacrale

CB   - Cranial breadth = greatest breadth across the Partes glutaeae
          of the ilia (+)

SB   - KB (German) - Smallest breadth of the Partes glutaeae (+)

AA   - Breadth between the borders of the acetabula, measured at the
          narrowest part (+)

DiA   - DA (German) - Diameter of one acetabulum: greatest distance
          including the Labium acetabuli (-)

BA   - Breadth in the middle: breadth across the two antitrochanter (+)

Points on and parts of the pelvis (Fig. 59):

             1 = Margo iliocranialis
             2 = Spina iliocaudalis
             3 = Pars glutaea
             4 = Antitrochanter
             5 = Os lumbosacrale
             6 = Vertebra thoracosynsacralis
             7 = Vertebrae caudales

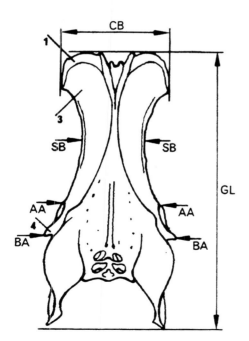

Figure 59d:
Pelvis
of <u>Buteo</u>,
dorsal view.

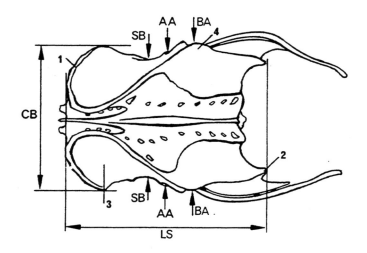

Figure 59e: Pelvis of <u>Columba</u>, dorsal view.

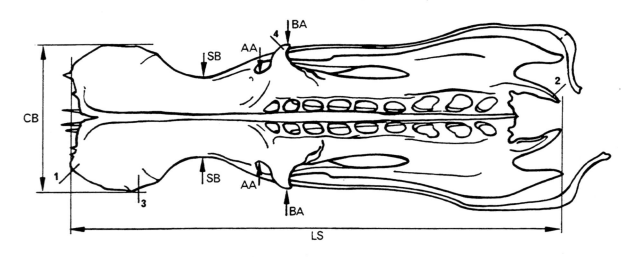

Figure 59f: Pelvis of <u>Phalacrocorax</u>, dorsal view.

FEMUR (Fig. 60a-c)

GL – Greatest length (+)

Lm – medial length (+)

Bp – (Greatest) breadth of the proximal end: Caput femoris – most
lateral point of the Trochanter major (–)*

Dp – Tp (German) – (Greatest) depth of the proximal end. The fixed points
for one calliper of the measuring instrument are the cranial
points on the Caput femoris and on the Trochanter major.*

SC – KC (German) – Smallest breadth of the corpus. Measured in the same
plane as Bd (–)**

Bd – (Greatest) breadth of the distal end (+)

Dd – Td (German) – (Greatest) depth of the distal end. The fixed points
for one calliper of the measuring instrument are the caudal points
of the Condyli lateralis and medialis.

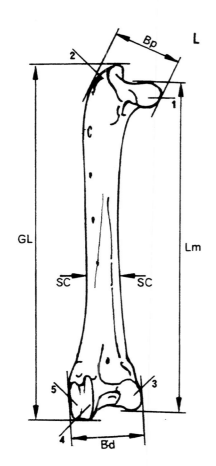

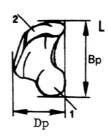

Figure 60b: Femur
of Gallus, proximal view.

Figure 60a:
Femur of Gallus,
caudal view.

Points on and parts of
the femur (Fig. 60):

1 = Caput femoris
2 = Trochanter major
3 = Condylus medialis
4 = Condylus lateralis
5 = Condylus fibularis

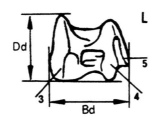

Figure 60c: Femur
of Gallus, distal view.

*Erbersdobler (1968, Fig. 9) designates the Bp as Dp – Durchmesser proximal (=proximal diameter) and the Dp as Bp – Breite proximal (=proximal breadth). This point should be noted when comparing literature which is based on Erbersdobler's data.

**See note to SC of the Humerus.

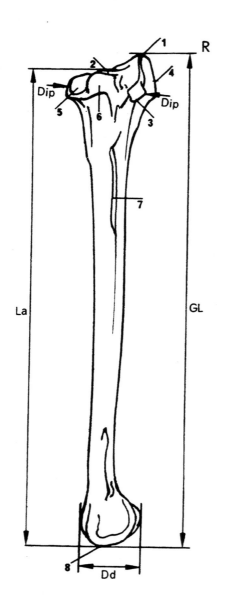

Figure 61a: Tibiotarsus of <u>Gallus</u>, lateral view.

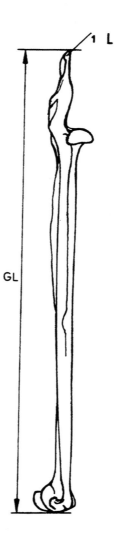

Figure 61b:
Tibiotarsus
of <u>Podiceps</u>,
lateral view.

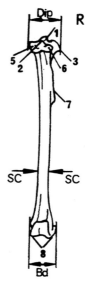

Figure 61c:
Tibiotarsus
of <u>Columba</u>,
plantar view.

GL – Greatest length. In the divers (Gaviidea and Podicipedidae) this measurement has to be measured in a fashion analogous to the other species (i.e., including the extremely long Processus cnemialis) (+)

La – Axial length: from the Tuberculum centrale to the distal border of the Trochlea tibiotarsi

Dip – Dp (German) – (Greatest) diagonal of the proximal end: from the Condylus medialis femoralis to the Crista lateralis, even though in some species the distance from the Condylus medialis femoralis to the Crista tibiae is greater (+)

SC – KC (German) – Smallest breadth of the corpus. Measured in the same plane as Bd (–)*

Bd – (Greatest) breadth of the distal end. (+)

Dd – Td (German) – Depth of the distal end. The fixed points for one calliper of the measuring instrument are the caudal points of the condyles (+)

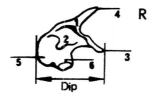

Figure 61d: Tibiotarsus of <u>Anser</u>, proximal view.

Points on and parts of the tibiotarsus (Fig. 61):

1 = Processus cnemialis
2 = Tuberculum centrale
3 = Crista lateralis
4 = Crista tibiae
5 = Condylus medialis femoralis
6 = Condylus lateralis femoralis
7 = Crista fibularis
8 = Trochlea tibiotarsi

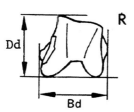

Figure 61e: Tibiotarsus of <u>Anser</u>, distal view.

*See note to SC of the Humerus.

TARSOMETATARSUS (Fig. 62a-c)

GL – Greatest length (+)
Bp – (Greatest) breadth of the proximal end (+)
SC – KC (German) – Smallest breadth of the corpus (+)*
Bd – (Greatest) breadth of the distal end. Measured in projection at
    right angles to the longitudinal axis of the bone.

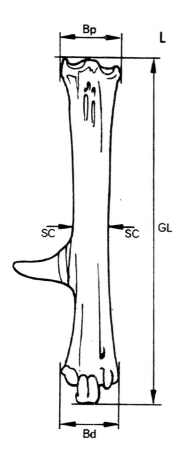

Figure 62a:
Tarsometatarsus
of <u>Gallus</u>,
dorsal view.

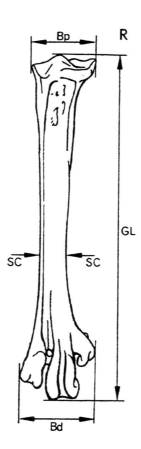

Figure 62b:
Tarsometatarsus
of <u>Anser</u>,
dorsal view.

Figure 62c:
Tarsometatarsus
of <u>Otis</u>,
dorsal view.

*See note to SC of the Humerus.

REFERENCES

Bacher, A.
1967   Vergleichend morphologische Untersuchungen an Einzelknochen
        des postkranialen Skeletts in Mitteleuropa vorkommender
        Schwäne und Gänse. Dissertation, Institut für Paläoanatomie,
        München.

Ballmann, P.
1966   Die Vögel aus der altburdigalen Spaltenfüllung von Wintershof
        (West) bei Eichstätt in Bayern. Dissertation, Institut für
        Paläontologie, München.

Bataller, R.
1952   "Estudio de los restos de animales procedentes de la Estación
        protohistórica de Cortes de Navarra," *Revista "Principe de
        Viana"*, vol.13, pp. 41-64. Pamplona.

1953   "Complemento al estudio de los restos de animales procedentes
        de la Estación protohistórica de Cortes de Navarra," *Revista
        "Principe de Viana"*, vol. 14, pp. 47-57. Pamplona.

Boessneck, J.
1969   "Zoologie im Dienst der Archäologie," *Archäologie und Biologie,*
        Forschungsberichte 15, pp. 48-56. Wiesbaden.

Boessneck, J. and T. Ciliga
1966   "Zu den Tierknochenfunden aus der Siedlung der römischen Kaiser-
        zeit auf dem 'Erbbrink' bei Seinstedt, Kreis Wolfenbüttel,"
        Neue Ausgrabungen und Forschungen in Niedersachsen, vol. 3,
        pp. 145-179. Hildesheim.

Boessneck, J. and A. von den Driesch
1967   "Die Tierknochenfunde aus dem fränkischen Reihengräberfeld in
        Kleinlangheim, Landkreis Kitzingen," *Zeitschrift für Säuge-
        tierkunde*, vol. 32, pp. 193-215.

1973   "Die jungpleistozänen Tierknochenfunde aus der Brillenhöhle,"
        in *Das Paläolithikum der Brillenhöhle bei Blaubeuren*, Teil II,
        edited by G. Riek. Stuttgart.

1976   "The Significance of Measuring Animal Bones from Archaeological
        Sites," in *Approaches to Faunal Analysis in the Middle East*,
        edited by R. H. Meadow and M.A. Zeder, in preparation.

Boessneck, J., A. von den Driesch, and N.-G. Gejvall
1968   "Die Knochenfunde von Säugetieren und vom Menschen," *The Arch-
        aeology of Skedemosse III*. Stockholm.

Boessneck, J., A. von den Driesch, U. Meyer-Lemppenau, & E. Wechsler von Ohlen
1971   "Die Tierknochenfunde aus dem Oppidum von Manching," *Die Ausgra-
        bungen in Manching*, vol. 6. Wiesbaden.

Boessneck, J. and M. Stork
1973   "Die Tierknochenfunde der Ausgrabungen 1959 auf der Wüstung
        Klein-Büddenstedt, Kreis Helmstedt," *Neue Ausgrabungen und
        Forschungen in Niedersachsen*, vol. 8, pp. 179-213. Hildesheim.

Brinkmann, A.
1924   "Canidenstudien V-VI," *Bergens Museums Aarbok* 1923/24.
        Naturvidenskabelig Raekke Nr. 7, pp. 1-57. Bergen.

Dahr, E.
1937   "Studien über Hunde aus primitiven Steinzeitkulturen in Nord-
        europa," *Lunds Universitets Årsskrift*, NF, Avd. 2, vol. 23,
        no. 4. Lund.

Degerbøl, M. and B. Fredskild
1970   *The Urus and Neolithic Domesticated Cattle in Denmark*, København.

Dolling, W. and H. Reichstein
1975   "Ein neues Gerät zum Vermessen zoologischer und archäologischer
        Objekte," in *Archaeozoological Studies*, edited by A.T. Clason,
        pp. 18-20. Amsterdam.

Dräger, N.
1964   "Tierknochenfunde aus der Stadt auf dem Magdalensberg bei Klagen-
        furt in Kärnten. I. Die Vogelknochen," Dissertation, München,
        1964.-& *Kärntner Museumsschriften*, vol. 33. Klagenfurt, 1964.

Driesch, A. von den
1972   "Osteoarchäologische Untersuchungen auf der Iberischen Halbinsel,"
        Studien über frühe Tierknochenfunde von der Iberischen Halbinsel,
        vol. 3, pp. 1-267. München.

Driesch, A. von den and J. Boessneck
1970   "Vorgeschichtliche Kaninchen aus zwei südspanischen Siedlungs-
        hügeln," *Säugetierkundliche Mitteilungen*, vol. 18, pp. 127-151.

Ducos, P.
1967   "Les Equidés des Tombes Royales de Salamine," in *Excavations in
        the Necropolis of Salamis* I by V. Karageorghis, pp. 154-181.
        Nicosia, Cyprus.

Duerst, J. U.
1926   "Vergleichende Untersuchungsmethoden am Skelett bei Säugern,"
        in *Handbuch der biologischen Arbeitsmethoden*, Abt. 7: Methoden
        der vergleichenden morphologischen Forschung, Heft 2, pp. 125-
        530. Berlin & Wien.

Ellenberger, W. and H. Baum
1943   *Handbuch der vergleichenden Anatomie der Haustiere*. 18. Aufl.
        Berlin.

Erbersdobler, K.
1968   Vergleichend morphologische Untersuchungen an Einzelknochen
        des postcranialen Skeletts in Mitteleuropa vorkommender
        mittelgrosser Hühnervögel. Dissertation, Institut für Paläo-
        anatomie, München.

Fick, O.
1974   Vergleichend morphologische Untersuchungen an Einzelknochen
        europäischer Taubenarten. Dissertation, Institut für Paläo-
        anatomie, München.

Gejvall, N.-G.
1973   "Automation och arkeoosteologi," TOR 1972/1973, vol. 17, pp.
        257-262. Stockholm.

Haltenorth, T. and W. Trense
1956   *Das Grosswild der Erde und seine Trophäen*. Bonn, München, & Wien.

Hauser, M.
1921   *Osteologische Unterscheidungsmerkmale der schweizerischen
        Feld- und Alpenhasen (Lepus europaeus Pall. und Lepus medius
        varronis Miller)*. Leipzig.

Hole, F. and K.V. Flannery
1962   "Faunal Remains. Excavations in Ali Kosh, Iran 1961," *Iranica
        Antiqua*, vol. 2, pp. 126-134. Leipzig.

Hole, F., K.V. Flannery, and J.A. Neely
1969   "Prehistory and Human Ecology of the Deh Luran Plain. An Early
        Village Sequence from Khuzistan, Iran," *Memoirs of the Museum
        of Anthropology, University of Michigan*, vol. 1. Ann Arbor.

Hornberger, M.
1970   "Gesamtbeurteilung der Tierknochenfunde aus der Stadt auf dem
        Magdalensberg in Kärnten (1948-1966)," Dissertation, München,
        1969.-& *Kärntner Museumsschriften*, vol. 49. Klagenfurt, 1970.

Ingebrigtsen, O.
1924   "Das norwegische Rotwild," *Bergens Museums Aarbok* 1922/23.
        Naturvidenskabelig Raekke, pp. 1-242. Bergen.

Iregren, E. and R. Jonsson
1973   "Hur ben krymper vid kremering," *Fornvännen Art.*, vol. 68, pp.
        97-100. Stockholm.

Kiesewalter, L.
1888   Skelettmessungen an Pferden als Beitrag zur theoretischen
        Beurteilungslehre des Pferdes. Dissertation, Leipzig.

Kleinschmidt, A.
1956   "Über das neuere Vorkommen von Wölfen in Niedersachsen (ab 1800
        bis heute)," in *Natur und Jagd in Niedersachsen*, edited by
        Steininger, pp. 38-62. Hildesheim & Hannover.

Kraft, E.
1972 Vergleichend morphologische Untersuchungen an Einzelknochen nord- und mitteleuropäischer kleinerer Hühnervogel. Dissertation, Institut für Paläoanatomie, München.

Kratochvil, Z.
1973 "Schädelkriterien der Wild- und Hauskatze (*Felis silvestris silvestris* Schreb. 1777 und *F. s. f. catus* L. 1758), *Acta Scientiarum Naturalium Brno* n.s. vol. 7, no. 10, pp. 1-50. Prag.

Kühnhold, B.
1971 Die Tierknochenfunde aus Unterregenbach, einer mittelalterlichen Siedlung Württenbergs. Dissertation, Institut für Paläoanatomie, München.

Küpper, W.
1972 Die Tierknochenfunde von der Burg Schiedberg bei Sagogn in Graubünden. II. Die kleinen Wiederkäuer, die Wildtiere und das Geflügel. Dissertation, Institut für Paläoanatomie, München.

Kuhn, E.
1932 "Beiträge zur Kenntnis der Säugetierfauna der Schweiz seit dem Neolithikum," *Revue Suisse de Zoologie*, vol. 39, pp. 531-768.

Leithner, O. von
1927 "Der Ur," *Bericht der internationalen Gesellschaft zur Erhaltung des Wisents*, vol. 2. Berlin.

Lesbre, M.F.X.
1903 "Recherches anatomiques sur les Camélidés," *Archives du Muséum d'Histoire naturelle de Lyon*, vol. 8, pp. 1-195. Lyon.

Martín-Roldán, R.
1959 "Estudio anatómico de los restos óseos procedentes de las excavaciones arqueológicas en el Cerro 'El Carambolo' (Sevilla)," *Anales de la Universidad Hispalense*, vol. 19, pp. 11-47.

Müller, R.
1967 Die Tierknochen aus den spätrömischen Siedlungsschichten von Lauriacum. II. Wild- und Haustierknochen ohne die Rinder. Dissertation, Institut für Paläoanatomie, München.

Nickel, R., A. Schummer, and E. Seiferle
1961 *Lehrbuch der Anatomie der Haustiere*, Bd. 1 Bewegungsapparat. 2. Aufl. Berlin & Hamburg.

Perkins, D.
1964 "The prehistoric fauna from Shanidar, Iraq," *Science*, vol. 144, pp. 1565-1566.

Pira, A.
1909 "Studien zur Geschichte der Schweinerassen, insbesondere derjenigen Schwedens," *Zoologische Jahrbücher* Suppl. 10, pp. 233-426.

Reed, C.A.
1960   "A review of the archaeological evidence on animal domestication in the prehistoric Near East," in "Prehistoric Investigations in Iraqi Kurdistan," *Studies in Ancient Oriental Civilization* No. 31, edited by R.J. Braidwood and B. Howe, pp. 119-145, Chicago.

Reitsma, G.G.
1932   *Zoologisch Onderzoek der Nederlandsche Terpen*. 1. Teil Het Schaap. Wageningen.

1935   *Zoologisch Onderzoek der Nederlandsche Terpen*. 2. Teil Het Varken. Wageningen.

Romer, A.S.
1971   *Vergleichende Anatomie der Wirbeltiere*. 3. Aufl. Hamburg & Berlin.

Sauer-Neubert, A.
1969   Tierknochenfunde aus der römischen Zivilsiedlung in Hüfingen. II. Wild- und Haustierknochen mit Ausnahme der Rinder. Dissertation, Institut für Paläonatomie, München.

Schmid, E.
1972   *Atlas of Animal Bones. Knochenatlas für Prähistoriker, Archäologen und Quartärbiologen*. Amsterdam, London, & New York.

Schülke, H.
1965   "Die Tierknochenfunde von der Burg-Neuschellenberg, Fürstentum Liechtenstein," *Jahrbuch des Historisches Vereins für das Fürstentum Liechtenstein*, vol. 64, pp. 177-262. Vaduz.

Schweizer, W.
1961   "Zur Frühgeschichte des Haushuhns in Mitteleuropa," *Studien an vor- und frühgeschichtlichen Tierresten Bayerns*, vol. 9, München.

Silver, I.A.
1963   "The Ageing of Domestic Animals," in *Science in Archaeology*, edited by D. Brothwell and E. Higgs, pp. 250-268. London.

Sisson, S. and J.D. Grossman
1950   *The Anatomy of the Domestic Animals*. 4th edition. Philadelphia & London.

Szunyoghy, J.
1963   *Das ungarische Rotwild*. Budapest.

Uerpmann, H.-P.
1971   "Die Tierknochenfunde aus der Talayotsiedlung von S'Illot, San Lorenzo/Mallorca," Dissertation, München, 1970, -& *Studien über frühe Tierknochenfunde von der Iberischen Halbinsel*, vol. 2. München, 1971.

Wagner, K.
    1930   "Rezente Hunderassen. Eine osteologische Untersuchung," *Skrifter
            utgitt av det Norske Videnskaps-Akademi i Oslo* 1929, vol. 3,
            no. 9. Oslo.

Woelfle, E.
    1967   Vergleichend morphologische Untersuchungen an Einzelknochen des
            postcranialen Skeletts in Mitteleuropa vorkommender Enten, Halb-
            gänse und Säger. Dissertation, Institut für Paläoanatomie,
            München.

Zietzschmann, O.
    1924   *Lehrbuch der Entwicklungsgeschichte der Haustiere.* Berlin 1924.
            2 Aufl.: Zietzschmann, O. and O. Krölling. Berlin & Hamburg, 1955.

ADDENDA

on the occasion of the first reprinting

to page 47: *Measurements of the cranium of Felis*

(12a)   Length: aboral border of the alveolus of M^1 - Prosthion.
          Not shown in Fig. 17 (-)

(12b)   Length: aboral border of the alveolus of M^1 - oral border of the
          canine alveolus. Not shown in Fig. 17 (+)

to page 61: *Measurements of the mandible of Canis*

Note: Measurements nos. 22, 23, 24, 25, and 26 are to be calculated only
        for specimens of domestic dog (Canis familiaris).

1 November 1977

on the occasion of the second reprinting

to page 61: *Measurements of the mandible of Canis*

(7a)   Length: aboral border of the alveolus of M_3 - oral border of the
          canine alveolus. Not shown in Fig. 23. Wild canids only.

22 December 1980

on the occasion of the fifth reprinting

The following measurements on horses are no longer necessary to be taken:

    Humerus GL1 (p. 77)
    Radius and Ulna GL1 (p. 79)
    Radius L1 (p. 79)
    Tibia L1 (p. 87)
    Metapodial L1 (p. 93) following Kiesewalter (1888).

Kiesewalter's work on the calculation of withers height in horses was found
to contain a series of discrepancies by May (1985), who uses the Greatest
Length of the respective parts of the skeleton for his calculations.

to page 134: Insert the following reference:

May, E.
  1985 "Widerristhöhe und Langknochen bei Pferden: ein immer noch
        aktuelles Problem." *Zeitschrift für Säugetierkunde,* vol. 50, pp.
        368-382.

26 August 1999